FAITHFUL
Celebrations

MAKING TIME WITH FAMILY AND FRIENDS

Edited by

SHARON ELY PEARSON

CHURCH
PUBLISHING
INCORPORATED

Scripture texts referred to in this work are taken from the *New Revised Standard Version Bible*, copyright © 1989 by the Division of Christian Education of the National Council of Churches of Christ in the USA, and are used by permission.

Acknowledgments: Faithful Celebrations is the work of many unnamed contributors, as well as Carolyn Chilton, Janie Stevens, Dina Strong, Sylvia DeVillers, Sara Fontana, Kathy Finely, Rita Mailander, Kathy Coffey, Dirk deVries, Sharon Ely Pearson, and Jim Wahler.

Illustrators: Sally Brewer Lawrence, Anne Kosel, Victoria Bergesen, Tom Lybeck, and Paula Becker

Church Publishing
19 East 34th Street
New York, NY 10016
www.churchpublishing.org

Cover design by Jennifer Kopec, 2Pug Design
Typeset by Rose Design

A record of this book is available from the Library of Congress.

ISBN-13: 978-1-64065-093-0 (pbk.)
ISBN-13: 978-1-64065-094-7 (ebook)

Printed in Canada

Contents

Contents

Introduction

But speaking the truth in love, we must grow up in every way into him who is the head, into Christ, from whom the whole body, joined and knit together by every ligament with which it is equipped, as each part is working properly, promotes the body's growth in building itself up in love.

—Ephesians 4:15–16

In a small way, this book's intention is to help the Body of Christ grow in understanding and "build itself up through love" at church or home. Celebrations, gatherings, and rituals help members of every generation find both individual meaning and common ground, all through the medium of direct experience, no matter the age of the participant. *Faithful Celebrations: Making Time with Family and Friends* offers a multitude of ideas for planning an event focused on a secular day that occurs during the spring and summer months (in the northern hemisphere) that will bring families together and build strong communities of faith, whether it is in the home or a congregational setting. Since family relationships and community togetherness occur both inside and outside of a church setting, the celebrations within these pages come from secular or popular culture roots as opposed to religious seasons and holidays. These are offered from the perspective of, "How does this occasion relate to my Christian faith?"

Through such occasions we can become better acquainted with our extended family—young and old together—in any setting. We can take steps toward making our congregation (or neighborhood) the warm, nurturing community we long for in our fragmented world. Older adults sometimes feel a sense of displacement in congregational life today, and younger people are increasingly looking to a variety of sources for spiritual nurture and faith practice. Singing, praying, eating, and creating memories together enhances our well-being and makes our connections to one another stronger. Undergirding our experiences is the presence of God among us, nurturing us and working through us to help us grow in the knowledge and love of Christ Jesus.

Through community celebrations, we can experience scripture and traditions in a fresh way that can give beauty and meaning to our daily lives. Within these pages you will find ideas to hold a theme-based event, or simply ideas to supplement other activities you have planned. This abundance allows you to choose only those activities that meet your congregation's or family's particular needs—and fit your timeframe. *Faithful Celebrations* will help you and your family—at home, school, or church—learn more and experience these particular spring and summer holidays and occasions:

- Earth Day
- Cinco de Mayo
- Mother's Day
- Memorial Day
- Father's Day
- Summer Solstice
- 4th of July
- Summer Celebration of God's Creation

ALL AGES GROWING TOGETHER

Many of the formative experiences in life happen when several generations are together. In our society we tend to separate people by ages mainly for education and employment. In recent years, Christian formation programs have made this same separation of generations, but more and more religious educators are recommending programs in which adults and children learn together. It is a way to pass on faith—generation to generation. Old learn from young, and young learn from old.

Faithful Celebrations is designed to meet the need for generations to learn together. This approach requires that we venture beyond traditional learning methods into the world of experiential learning. Just as old and young alike can participate in vacations, trips, holidays, and family events together, learning more about our relationship with God can take place with all generations growing together. This may mean that adults work alongside children, helping them as well as listening to them as full partners in an activity or discussion. It means allowing children to experience things for themselves, not doing things for them but with them.

WHEN, WHERE, WHY, AND HOW

Finding time and resources to add another component to already full schedules, both in families and in congregations, can be a challenge. Within your community of faith, look to different groups who could successfully host an intergenerational gathering. One promising lead might be to invite your youth organization to be in charge of leading one or more sessions. Consider also the possibility of asking different congregational organizations to host a given session. In a typical community of faith, consider using these ideas as:

- intergenerational and multi-age programming
- seasonal church gatherings for families
- primary Christian education material for a small church
- supplementary material for large Christian education programs
- supplementary material for classes in church-based schools
- home study Christian education programs
- small-community or base-community Christian education
- supplementary material for family sacramental programs

In a home setting, families can use these activities for:

- family vacations and holidays
- neighborhood or community events

- home schooling and education
- gatherings of friends and families

Each chapter in *Faithful Celebrations* begins with an Introduction that includes background material and key ideas for each celebration. Use this content to inspire your vision of what the event needs to be, for you, your planning committee, and your congregation or family. The pages that follow are organized by type of activity, such as opening prayer, story, craft, food, drama, music, game, or more. It will always conclude with a closing activity of prayer.

Each activity or experience will include a very brief explanation for the leader, followed by a list of materials needed and step-by-step directions. The materials called for in this book are simple and inexpensive. Those common to most activities are:

- Bibles
- whiteboard, poster board, or newsprint pad with markers
- felt pens
- crayons (regular and oversized for young children)
- drawing paper
- glue
- scissors

From time to time links will be offered to supplemental online materials; there are also downloadable resources of craft patterns and templates available for free at *www.churchpublishing.org/ faithfulcelebrations5*.

> O God, you have filled the world with beauty: Open our eyes to behold your gracious hand in all your works; that, rejoicing in your whole creation, we may learn to serve you with gladness; for the sake of him through whom all things were made, your Son Jesus Christ our Lord. *Amen.*[1]

---

1. "For Joy in God's Creation" in the Book of Common Prayer, 814.

Chapter 1

EARTH DAY

INTRODUCTION

We celebrate Earth Day each year to focus our attention on environmental concerns and activities. As Christians we can respond to our call to seek and serve Christ in all persons loving our neighbor as ourselves through care of the environment.

The History of Earth Day

In the spring of 1962, Rachel Carson wrote the classic book *Silent Spring* (New York: Houghton Mifflin Company, 2002). The book represented a watershed moment for the modern environmental movement, selling more than 500,000 copies in 24 countries. In 1970, the first Earth Day was celebrated building on the energy of the antiwar protest movement to put environmental concerns out in the open. Gaylord Nelson, a U.S. senator from Wisconsin, called for the people of the world to celebrate the earth on April 22. Over 20 million people participated that year, and now over 500 million people and governments in over 175 countries celebrate the earth on April 22.

The former Archbishop of Canterbury Rowan Williams has said, "Every Sunday in the creed, Christians confess their faith in God who created the world we inhabit. It's God's gift. As stewards of that gift, each of us has a responsibility, both to God and to generations to come, to ensure that this remains a sustainable world. Placing environmental concerns at the heart of our Christian worship for this fixed time each year demonstrates our shared commitment to this end."

The attention of the Church to environmental concerns is not limited to Earth Day. We celebrate Arbor Day in January and Rogation days in spring and fall as isolated events. Many churches around the world are developing a season of creation, the period of October through November (beginning with St. Francis' Day on October 4 and ending with Thanksgiving in late November). The Sunday lectionary readings reflect this season of creation and give a longer time period in which to address environmental issues and the churches' call to protect our earth.

In Eucharistic Prayer C of the Episcopal Church, we pray for this "fragile earth, our island home." We cannot afford to be passive observers or determined misusers of this, our home. Many prayers across our denominational spectrum address the concerns for environment and for proper use of the gifts that God has given us, and many hymns carry this theme as well.

The Sustainable Development Goals

In 2000 the United Nations launched the Millennium Development Goals (MDGs), eight goals with measurable targets and clear deadlines for improving the lives of the world's poorest people. Leaders of 189 countries signed the historic millennium declaration at the United Nations Millennium Summit in 2000. These goals ranged from halving extreme poverty rates to halting the spread of HIV/AIDS and providing universal primary education, all by the target date of 2015.

From the momentum generated by the MDGs and to carry on with an ambitious post-2015 development agenda, the United Nations launched the Sustainable Development Goals in 2015. They are a call for action by all countries—poor, rich, and middle-income—to promote prosperity while protecting the planet. They recognize that ending poverty must go hand-in-hand with strategies that build economic growth and address a range of social needs including education, health, social protection, and job opportunities, while tackling climate change and environmental protection. These Goals interconnect and in order to leave no one behind, the United Nations desires to achieve each Goal and target by 2030.

1. *No Poverty*—Donate what you don't use.
2. *Zero Hunger*—Avoid throwing away food.
3. *Good Health and Well-Being*—Vaccinate your family to protect them and improve public health.
4. *Quality Education*—Help children in your community to read.
5. *Gender Equality*—Call out sexist language and behavior.
6. *Clean Water and Sanitation*—Avoid wasting water.
7. *Affordable and Clean Energy*—Use only energy efficient appliances and lightbulbs.
8. *Decent Work and Economic Growth*—Buy from green companies that are equal opportunity employers.
9. *Industry, Innovation, and Infrastructure*—Think of innovative new ways to repurpose old material.
10. *Reduce Inequalities*—Raise your voice against discrimination.
11. *Sustainable Cities and Communities*—Bike, walk, or use public transportation to keep our cities' air clean.
12. *Responsible Production and Consumption*—Recycle paper, plastic, glass, and aluminum.
13. *Climate Action*—Educate young people on climate change to put them on a sustainable path early on.
14. *Life Below Water*—Avoid plastic bags to keep the oceans safe and clean.
15. *Life on Land*—Plant a tree and help protect the environment.
16. *Peace, Justice, and Strong Institutions*—Use your right to elect the leaders in your country and local community.
17. *Partnership for the Goals*—Get the SDGs in Action app to learn about the Goals and ways to help achieve them! (*www.SDGs inaction.com*)

As you can see, many of these goals are tied to caring for God's creation. Within this celebration you will find many ideas to begin conversation on these goals as they relate to our faith. Many are listed specifically in the Faith in Action section beginning on page 19.

Beyond the Celebration

Earth Day offers many opportunities to interact with the world around us and care for "our island home." Instead of having a celebration that lasts just one day, strategize how your congregation, family, or neighborhood can take some of these ideas to heart in changing lifestyles and practices at home and church every day of the year.

WORSHIP

Opening Prayers

Choose from this selection of prayers from the Book of Common Prayer to use at the beginning or throughout this celebration.

Almighty God, in giving us dominion over things on earth, you made us fellow workers in your creation: Give us wisdom and reverence so to use the resources of nature, that no one may suffer from our abuse of them, and that generations yet to come may continue to praise you for your bounty; through Jesus Christ our Lord. *Amen.*[1]

Almighty God, whose loving hand has given us all that we possess: Grant us grace that we may honor you with our substance, and, remembering the account which we must one day give, may be faithful stewards of your bounty, through Jesus Christ our Lord. *Amen.*[2]

Almighty and everlasting God, you made the universe with all its marvelous order, its atoms, worlds, and galaxies, and the infinite complexity of living creatures: Grant that, as we probe the mysteries of your creation, we may come to know you more truly, and more surely fulfill our role in your eternal purpose; in the name of Jesus Christ our Lord. *Amen.*[3]

O gracious Father, who opens your hand and fills all things living with plenteousness: Bless the land and waters, and multiply the harvests of the world; let your Spirit go forth, that it may renew the face of the earth; show your loving-kindness, that our land may give her increase; and save us from selfish use of what you give, that men and women everywhere may give you thanks; through Christ our Lord. *Amen.*[4]

---

1. "For the Conservation of Natural Resources" in the Book of Common Prayer, 827.
2. "For the Right Use of God's Gifts" in the Book of Common Prayer, 827.
3. "For Knowledge of God's Creation" in the Book of Common Prayer, 827.
4. "For the Harvest of Lands and Waters" in the Book of Common Prayer, 828.

CRAFTS

A Song of Creation Booklet (or Mural or Tablecloth)

Canticle 12, "A Song of Creation," is the prayer of thanksgiving prayed by Shadrach, Meshach, and Abednego after they were saved from the fiery furnace in the Book of Daniel. The Invocation, The Cosmic Order, The Earth and Its Creatures, and The People of God comprise the sections. It is a beautiful hymn of praise and particularly in celebration of the earth.

Materials

- sheets of sturdy 8½" x 11" drawing paper, 3 per participant
- long-reach stapler
- markers
- crayons
- colored pencils
- old magazines and newspapers
- scissors
- glue or glue sticks
- tape
- copies of "A Song of Creation" download at *www.church publishing.org/faithfulcelebrations5*, or copies of the Book of Common Prayer (p. 88)

Directions

1. Distribute Canticle 12 (I and II) of "The Song of Creation" to participants.
2. Read the canticle together or with a variety of voices reading different stanzas.
3. Discuss the meaning and context of the canticle from the description above. (You may also want to share the story of "The Fiery Furnace" from Daniel 3:1–30.)

4. Distribute 3 sheets of drawing paper to each participant. Explain:

- Fold all of your sheets together and staple on the crease.
- Now you have a booklet with 12 pages.
- The front page is the cover. On the inside front page write your name.
- Write the petitions of "A Song of Creation" on pages of your booklet.
- Illustrate each stanza by drawing, painting, or cutting pictures or words from magazines or newspapers.
- Use your prayer booklet in your family devotions.

Alternatives

- Together create a mural to put on the wall, including the words of "A Song of Creation." For this you'll need a strip of butcher paper or newsprint, tape or tacks, and the other materials listed above.
- Together create a tablecloth for your celebration meal. Start with a long strip of butcher paper or paper tablecloth and make available the materials listed above. Again, include the words of "A Song of Creation," and invite group members to decorate the tablecloth as they wish.

Suncatchers

What do you do with unwanted CDs that clutter up your home, office, or kitchen counter? Turn them into a fun upcycling project that will add sparkle indoors or out!

Materials

- junk CDs
- craft glue
- things that sparkle or are colorful (rhinestones, beads, glitter, sequins, etc.)
- fishing line
- scissors
- newspaper

Advance preparation

1. Cover your work surface with newspaper.
2. Plastic isn't the easiest surface when it comes to gluing things down. Test the glue on one CD by gluing a rhinestone or one of the larger, heavier decorations in place. If this glue works, let the artists begin! If not, try a different glue.

Directions

1. Give each participant a CD and let them get creative with the decorations. Create sparkly designs, styling the suncatchers with flowers, suns, or faces. Or create abstract patterns.
2. Let the glue dry.
3. When the glue has dried, pick up the suncatcher and be ready to catch anything that wasn't glued down. Reglue anything that isn't secure if you want. Again, let it dry.
4. Turn the disk over and decorate the second side. Again, let the glue dry and follow step 3.
5. Cut a two-foot length of the fishing line and tie it through the disk.
6. Hang the suncatcher indoors or outside for others to admire. Only hang it outside if you have used a glue that's not water soluble.

NATURE ACTIVITIES

Grow a Sock Garden

How many times have you caught your children walking outside with white socks on? In this activity, everyone has your permission to get their socks nice and filthy. Between dandelions, clover, plants, flowers, grass, and weeds, most yards are full of seeds. They're just not always apparent to the naked eye.

Materials

- pair of old cotton socks (preferably white), 1 pair per person
- magnifying glasses
- pencil and paper (or notebooks)
- crayons or markers
- small flower pots
- potting soil
- water for watering

Directions

1. Invite everyone to put on a pair of socks and walk around the front or backyard to pick up debris. Encourage them to walk through the grass, between plants, and through the flowerbeds (but not on the flowers!). Hopefully, everyone's socks will "pick up" lots of neat items.

2. When they are tired of walking around, ask everyone to carefully remove their socks. Use the magnifying glasses to take a look at what the socks have collected. Try to guess which seeds you see and ask them to predict what might grow. Direct them to write down their answers.

3. Then place the socks in small flowerpots, add some potting soil, and water lightly.

4. Everyone can take their "sock garden" home to watch what happens.

5. Encourage them to spend some time each day over the next days and weeks looking at the sock garden to see what grows! They can record their observations throughout this project.

Gardening

Materials

- tree seedlings
- shrubs
- vegetable seeds

Directions

1. Plant tree seedlings (with permission) in your community. Organize such a planting and then ongoing care for the new plants.
2. Plant shrubs in your own garden that attract birds or butterflies. Consider the watering needs of your lawn and garden. Can you make some changes in the way in which you water or how much you water?
3. Depending on your climate zone, plant some vegetables in your flowerbeds. You don't need huge amounts of land to have a garden. You can even plant some vegetables in pots. Then eat and enjoy your produce.

STORYTELLING AND BIBLE STUDY

Creation Care Bible Study

Choose from the following scriptures, as appropriate for your group. Note that some stories will be appropriate for all ages; some may be challenging even for older participants. You could also consider reading a chosen story to younger participants from a children's Bible, including one with illustrations.

Materials

- Bibles
- Select from one or more of the following scriptures:
    - Matthew 22:34–40: This is Jesus' response when asked about the important commandment.
    - Genesis 1–2: The creation story
    - Ecclesiastes 3:1ff: "To everything there is a season . . ."

Directions

1. Provide Bibles for participants.
2. Ask a volunteer (or volunteers) to read aloud the chosen scripture passage or story.
3. If you read Matthew 22:34–40, discuss:
    - What does Jesus say is the first commandment?
    - What does Jesus say is the second commandment?
    - Is there a connection between loving your neighbor and taking care of the environment? Explain.
    - How do we fail to keep the commandment "do unto others as you would have them do unto you" with respect to caring for the environment?
4. For the Genesis reading, discuss:
    - Where do you see the creation story fitting into today's celebration?

5. If you read the reading from Ecclesiastes:

   • How do you see it fitting into today's reading?

6. No matter which of the three readings you read, where do you find yourself?

7. Read the Sustainable Development Goals (see page 3). How does the passage (or do the passages) we read fit into these goals?

Exploring Children's Literature

Choose one or more of the books listed below from your local, school, or church library or from someone's personal library. Most of the books listed are appropriate for children in grades 3–5 and older. All of these are related to God's creation and the care of our environment.

• *Agatha's Feather Bed* by Carmen Deedy
• *The Lorax* by Dr. Seuss
• *A Prayer for the Earth* by Sandy Eisenberg Sasso
• *Song of Creation* by Paul Goble
• *Michael Recycle* by Ellie Bethel
• *Every Day Is Earth Day* by Kathy Ross
• *The Big Book for Our Planet* by Ann Durrell, Jean Craighead George, and Katherine Paterson
• *Keepers of the Earth: Native American Stories and Environmental Activities for Children* by Michael J. Caduto and Joseph Bruchac
• *Wangari's Trees of Peace: A True Story from Africa* by Jeanette Winter

Directions

1. Choose one of the books listed to read as a group.

2. Discuss the following questions:

   • What did you learn from this book? Did you learn something new?

- What does the book tell us about God's creation? our place in God's creation? how to take care of God's creation?
- What could you do differently because you read this book?
- Does this book remind you of other stories?
- Would you like to draw a picture about the book that you studied?
- Do you have a favorite book on this subject that was not listed above? Talk about it. Read it as a family when you get home.

3. If you read *Agatha's Feather Bed* by Carmen Deedy, discuss:

- "Everything comes from something. Nothing comes from nothing."
- Name places where things like linen, cotton, wool, etc. come from. How do we get these things?
- Who makes these things into items we can use?
- What did Agatha do when she realized that something she had purchased had implications upon someone else?
- What would you have done if you had been in Agatha's position? What if you didn't have long hair? What could you have done instead?

4. If you read *The Lorax* by Dr. Seuss, discuss:

- "Unless someone like you cares a whole awful lot, nothing is going to get better. It's not."
- Everything we do impacts others.
- We need to ask questions—the right kind of questions—that make us realize that we are destroying our world. Do you want a particular thing, or do you need it?
- What happened to the truffula trees? the brown barba-loots?
- If you were the "once-ler" what would you have done differently to protect the environment?
- What can we do today to protect the environment?

MUSIC

Incorporate music at any point in your Earth Day celebration. Below are a selection of familiar hymns celebrating God's creation.

Materials

- *The Hymnal 1982* or another hymnal with the songs listed below (or similar songs)
- piano or other instrument to accompany singing

Possible songs

- "For the Beauty of the Earth" #416
- "Earth and All Stars" #412
- "All Things Bright and Beautiful" #405
- "O Beautiful for Spacious Skies" #719

DRAMA

Film Festival

Depending on the age span of your participants, choose from one or more of the films or television shows to watch and discuss. Make certain you have permission to view the film in a church setting. To show films in a church setting, you must have a Church Video License. *Visit www.cvli.com.*

Materials

- one of the films selected from the list below
- a method of projecting and viewing the film (for example, computer with digital projector; large screen TV with DVD player)

Directions

1. Select a film from the list below.
2. Make sure the projection setup works and is ready to go.

Earth (Walt Disney Studios)

This Disney movie focuses on the earth and ecology. There are also short videos, a slideshow, and an Earth Educator's Guide available to help with your discussion, making these resources flexible for the timeframe of your celebration. *https://nature.disney.com/earth*

Planet Earth (BBC)

An eleven-episode series from the BBC, redone by the Discovery Channel in the United States. *www.discovery.com/tv-shows/planet-earth/*

Wall-E (Walt Disney Studios)

A delightful computer-animated film about friendship as well as the environment. Youth Specialties offers an online study guide with activities. *https://youthspecialties.com/blog/wall-e-movie-study/*

The Lorax (Warner Brothers)

This 2012 film adaptation of Dr. Seuss' book also has a study guide offered from Scholastic at *www.scholastic.com/teachers/lesson-plans/teaching-content/lorax-dr-seuss-lesson-plan/*

PRAYER ACTIVITIES

Write a Litany for Earth Day

A litany is a ceremonial or liturgical form of prayer. It consists of a series of invocations or supplications with responses that are the same for a number in succession. Create a group litany and use it in your celebration's concluding worship or a Sunday service.

Materials

- poster board or flip chart, with markers
- tape, tacks, or poster putty
- copies of the Book of Common Prayer

Directions

1. Divide the group into groups of 2 or 3 people. *Note:* Make sure that the diversity of the larger group is reflected in the smaller groups, including ages.
2. Look together at an example of a litany on page 836 of the Book of Common Prayer.
3. Invite the group to write a brief prayer for some aspect of Earth Day. The response can be the same after each prayer, for example, "We thank you Lord," "Help us, Good Lord," or some other appropriate response. Try to create a response that goes with the prayer. Keep the response the same for all the prayers.

GAMES

Recycle or Throw Away?

This activity can be done as a group or set up as a relay. Set up several stations around the room for participants to visit and sort recyclables. At each station they will sort the items into things that can be recycled and things that cannot. Individuals or teams can work at each station. Be creative in how you might imagine taking this concept of sorting to fit your context and the ages present.

Materials

- recycling bins or other containers (one per team)
- garbage bins or bags (one per team)
- items that are not recyclable (toys, real food, Styrofoam®, balloons, etc.)
- items that are recyclable (cans, bottles, cereal boxes, some plastics, etc.)
- *optional: Charlie and Lola: We Are Extremely Very Good Recyclers* by Lauren Child

Directions

1. *Optional*: Read *Charlie and Lola: We Are Extremely Very Good Recyclers* before playing the game.
2. Show participants a pile of items, some of which are recyclable and some are not.
3. Pick up a few of the items one at a time and ask whether or not they are recyclable. Ask students how they know (encourage them to look for the recycling symbol and to think about whether something is paper/plastic/glass).
4. Place a recycling bin and garbage can for each team on the other side of the room, with teams gathered opposite them. Have the pile of "trash" in the middle of the room on a tarp (since some of your items may be real trash).

5. As a relay race, individuals from each team should run to the pile, grab an item, and run to drop the item in the correct bin: recycle or garbage. They run back, tag the next person in line, who repeats the relay.

6. When all the teams are done, check the bins to make sure things are sorted correctly. Review why something might have been put in the wrong bin.

7. The group that has the most items placed in the correct bins wins.

Earth Day Musical Chairs

Turn the classic party game of musical chairs into a nature-themed game for Earth Day. All you have to do is modify some of the traditional game elements. For instance, instead of playing musical chairs, you can play musical lily pads.

Materials

- green construction paper
- scissors
- CD or MP3 player or other means to share music

Directions

1. Start by cutting green poster board into the shapes of lily pads, then place them in a line on the ground.

2. Instead of walking or running around the lily pads, kids can hop like frogs while the music plays. When the music stops, they jump onto a lily pad, instead of sitting in a chair.

3. The rest of the game is played as usual, where one lily pad is removed after each round until only one player remains.

FAITH IN ACTION

An Action Plan for Helping the Environment

Decide what you can do individually or as a community to help the environment. Invite individuals or families to create an action plan with stickers, check marks, or stars for keeping track of those jobs accomplished.

Materials

- blank calendar page(s) for each person (download at *www.church publishing.org/faithfulcelebrations5*)
- construction paper
- stickers
- magazines
- laminator or clear Contact® paper

Directions

1. Using a blank calendar template (one can be downloaded at *www.churchpublishing.org/faithfulcelebrations5*), make a copy for each person on 11" x 17" paper.

2. Laminate these pages (or cover them with clear Contact® paper) for each group member.

3. Give each person a piece of construction paper and stickers, magazines, etc. to help illustrate their list. Explain:

   - On the left side of your construction paper, list those things that you can do to help the environment.
   - Glue this page on the left-hand margin of your calendar page.
   - Each day that you do one of those things, put a sticker on your calendar page.
   - See how many stickers you can get at the end of the month.
   - To re-use your calendar page, write the days of the particular month on your calendar with a write-on/wipe-off pen. Pull off the old stickers to have room for new ones.

Suggestions

- Use your own refillable water bottle.
- Bring your own shopping bags to the grocery store or on other shopping errands.
- Use washable cloth bags for produce in the grocery store instead of plastic bags.
- Use washable containers to hold leftovers in the fridge rather than plastic bags.
- Collect rainwater to water potted plants.
- Pack your lunch in a nylon bag or other kind of reusable lunch box.
- Walk when possible rather than taking the car.
- Turn off lights when you are not using them.
- Turn off the tap while brushing your teeth.

A Billion Acts of Green

In 2010—the fortieth anniversary of Earth Day—the Earth Day Network launched *A Billion Acts of Green*. The goal of the campaign was to register one billion actions before the June 2012 United Nations Conference regarding Sustainable Development. When this first launched internationally, *Avatar* director James Cameron began a one-million-tree-planting initiative. The campaign reached the goal well before the conference took place.

When we come together, the impact can be monumental. Go green by making small changes that add up to making a big difference. Commit to earth-friendly acts, make more sustainable choices, re-duce your carbon foot-print, conserve energy and resources, collaborate on environmental projects in your community, vote for leaders committed to protect us and the environment, and share your acts of green to help educate and inspire others.

Directions

1. As a group discuss:

   - What could you do to add to the billion acts of green?
   - What could your church do to add to the billion acts of green?
   - Your community?

2. Here are some ideas and how they help care for the earth. (Learn more specifics at *www.earthday.org*.)

   - *Plant a tree or donate to plant a tree.* Deforestation contributes to species extinction, poverty, and is responsible for up to 15 percent of the global greenhouse gas emissions causing climate change. Planting trees is one of the easiest ways to fight climate change.
   - *Take the Pesticide Pledge.* Pledge to stop using pesticides and protect pollinators (butterflies and bees). *www.earthday.org/pesticide-pledge/*
   - *End plastic pollution.* Take personal responsibility for recycling and reducing your use of plastics that fill our landfills and pollute our oceans.
   - *Reduce your footprint.* Take the Ecological Footprint Quiz and learn how you can reduce your impact on the planet. *www.earthday.org/take-action/footprint-calculator/*

RECIPES

Earth and Worms

Ingredients

- 1 ready-made chocolate cake
- 1 box Oreo Cookie Crumbs
- 1 container chocolate ice cream
- 1 bag gummy worms

Supplies

- large bowl or small clear plastic cups (for individual servings)
- spoons

Directions

1. Put a slice of chocolate cake in the bottom of your dish.
2. Add some cookie crumbs.
3. Add a scoop or two of ice cream.
4. Add more cookie crumbs.
5. Top with gummy worms!

Ants on a Log

This is an old, easy favorite with a twist.

Ingredients

- 12 celery stalks, rinsed and trimmed
- 6 tablespoons chocolate-hazelnut spread
- dried cranberries
- semi-sweet mini chocolate kisses
- sunflower seeds

Directions

1. Fill the celery sticks with equal amounts of the chocolate-hazelnut spread.
2. Decorate the tops with "ants" in the form of the cranberries, chocolate pieces, and sunflower seeds.

WORSHIP

Concluding Worship

Choose one or more of these prayers to conclude your celebration. Sing one of the hymns found on page 14 or another popular song such as Pete Seeger's famous, "This Land Is Your Land."

> We give you thanks, most gracious God, for the beauty of earth and sky and sea; for the richness of mountains, plains and rivers; for the songs of birds and the loveliness of flowers. We praise you for these good gifts; and pray that we may safeguard them for our posterity. Grant that we may continue to grow in our grateful enjoyment of your abundant creation, to the honor and glory of your Name, now and for ever. *Amen.*[5]

> Cosmic Creator of all, we praise you for the scientific abilities that led to Rachel's groundbreaking research into the causes of water pollution. We also applaud her courage in giving up her government job so she was free to write about the necessity of caring for the Earth. Her contributions to the environmental movement and her sense of wonder at the beauty of creation encourage us to continue her work. Inspire us to put our respect for the Earth and, indeed, for the Universe into action. For we pray in the name of the Life-Giver. *Amen.*[6]

> Almighty God, giver of all good things: We thank you for the natural majesty and beauty of this land. They restore us, though we often destroy them. Heal us. We thank you for the great resources of this nation. They make us rich, though we often exploit them. Forgive us. *Amen.*[7]

---

5. "For the Beauty of the Earth" in the Book of Common Prayer, 840.

6. "A Prayer for Rachel Carson" in *She Who Prays, A Woman's Interfaith Prayer Book* (New York: Morehouse Publishing, 2005), 125.

7. Excerpted from "Thanksgiving for the Nation" in the Book of Common Prayer, 838.

Chapter 2

CINCO DE MAYO

INTRODUCTION

Cinco de Mayo (Spanish for "fifth of May") is celebrated nationwide in the United States and regionally in Mexico, primarily in the state of Puebla where the holiday is called *El Día de la Batalla de Puebla* (The Day of the Battle of Puebla). This date, May 5, is observed in the United States as a celebration of Mexican heritage and pride, and to commemorate the cause of freedom and democracy during the first years of the American Civil War. In the state of Puebla, the date is observed to commemorate the Mexican army's unlikely victory over French forces at the Battle of Puebla on May 5, 1862 under the leadership of General Ignacio Zaragoza Seguín. Contrary to widespread popular belief, Cinco de Mayo is not Mexico's Independence Day—the most important national patriotic holiday in Mexico.

In the United States Cinco de Mayo has taken on more significance than in Mexico. The date is perhaps best recognized in the United States as a date to celebrate the culture and experiences of Americans of Mexican ancestry, much as St. Patrick's Day, Oktoberfest, and the Chinese New Year are used to celebrate those of Irish, German, and Chinese ancestry, respectively. Similar to those holidays, many Americans, regardless of their ethnic origin, observe Cinco de Mayo. Celebrations tend to draw both from traditional Mexican symbols, such as the Virgin of Guadalupe, and from prominent figures of Mexican descent in the United States, including César Chávez.

Some Mexican history

Mexico declared its independence from Mother Spain on midnight, the fifteenth of September 1810. And it took eleven years before the first Spanish soldiers were told and forced to leave Mexico.

In 1861 the democratic Mexican Benito Juárez (1806–1872) became president of a country in financial ruin, and he was forced to default on his debts to European governments. In response, France, Britain, and Spain sent naval forces to Veracruz to demand reimbursement. Britain and Spain negotiated with Mexico and withdrew, but France, ruled by Napoleon III (1808–1873), decided to use the opportunity to carve a dependent empire out of Mexican territory.

Under Emperor Napoleon III, who detested the United States, the French came to stay. They installed Austrian Archduke Ferdinand Maximilian and his wife, Carlota, to rule their new Mexican empire. Napoleon's French Army had not been defeated in fifty years and it had the finest modern equipment and with a newly reconstituted Foreign Legion. The French were not afraid of anyone, especially since the United States was embroiled in its own Civil War.

Late in 1861, a well-armed French fleet stormed Veracruz, landing a large French force and driving President Juárez and his government into retreat. The French Army left the port of Vera Cruz to attack Mexico City to the west, as the French assumed that the Mexicans would give up should their capital fall to the enemy—as European countries traditionally did.

Certain that success would come swiftly, six thousand French troops under General Charles Latrille de Lorencez (1814–1892) set out to attack Puebla de Los Angeles, a small town in east-central Mexico. From his new headquarters in the north, Juárez rounded up a rag-tag force of two thousand loyal men—many of them either indigenous Mexicans or of mixed ancestry—and sent them to Puebla. Under the command of Texas-born General Ignacio Zaragoaza (1829–1862) and the cavalry under the command of Colonel Porfirio Díaz, the Mexicans waited for the French Army to attack. Brightly dressed French Dragoons led the enemy columns. The Mexican Army was less stylish.

General Zaragoza ordered Colonel Díaz to take his cavalry, the best in the world, out to the French flanks. In response, the French did a foolish thing; they sent their cavalry off to chase Díaz and his men, who proceeded to butcher them. The remaining French infantrymen charged the Mexican defenders through sloppy mud from a thunderstorm and through hundreds of head of stampeding cattle stirred up by Indians armed only with machetes. The battle lasted from daybreak to early evening, and when the French finally retreated, many had been killed or wounded. Their cavalry was being chased by Díaz's superb horsemen miles away.

Meanwhile, in the United States . . .

The Mexicans had won a great victory that kept Napoleon III from supplying the Confederacy from across the border for another year, allowing the United States to build the greatest army the world had ever seen. This grand army smashed the Confederates at Gettysburg just fourteen months after the battle of Puebla, essentially ending the Civil War.

Union forces were then rushed to the Texas/Mexican border under General Philip Sheridan, who made sure that the Mexicans got all the weapons and ammunition they needed to expel the French. Six years later—thanks in part to the military support and political pressure from the United States, which had finally ended its Civil War—France withdrew from Mexico. The American Legion of Honor marched in the Victory Parade in Mexico City. It might be a historical stretch to credit the survival of the United States to those brave four thousand Mexicans who faced an army twice as large in 1862. But who knows?

So, Why Cinco de Mayo?

And why should Americans savor this day as well? Because four thousand Mexican soldiers smashed the French and traitor Mexican army of eight thousand at Puebla, Mexico, one hundred miles east of Mexico City on the morning of May 5, 1862. In gratitude, thousands of Mexicans crossed the border after Pearl Harbor to join the U.S. Armed Forces. As recently as the Persian Gulf War, Mexicans flooded American consulates with phone calls, trying to join up and fight another war for America.

Mexicans, you see, never forget who their friends are and neither do Americans. That's why Cinco de Mayo is such a party—a party that celebrates freedom and liberty. These are the two ideals that Mexicans and Americans have fought shoulder to shoulder to protect, ever since the fifth of May 1862. VIVA! el CINCO DE MAYO!!

Let's celebrate!

Today, native Mexican (and American) people everywhere celebrate Cinco de Mayo to highlight Mexican culture, especially in its music and regional dancing.

In several towns in Mexico, on the fifth of May, along with many speeches and parades, the Battle of Puebla is elaborately reenacted in a whole-day dramatization. *Mariachi* bands play while dancers perform native Mexican dances such as the *baile folklórico* (folk dances) and *raspa* (Mexican Hat Dance). To celebrate, many display Cinco de Mayo banners while schools often hold special events to educate pupils about its historical significance.

In America, Cinco de Mayo is seen as an opportunity to celebrate Hispanic culture in general. This is done through huge fairs that include Mexican singing, dancing, feasting, costumes, sports activities, fireworks, and entertainment. Speeches and parades encompass a large part of the celebration too. Chicano activists raised awareness of the holiday in the 1960s, in part because they identified with the victory of indigenous Mexicans over European invaders during the Battle of Puebla. Some of the largest festivals are held in Los Angeles, Chicago, Denver, and Houston.

These events are one way in which people celebrate the friendship of the United States and Mexico. This observance of the Cinco de Mayo victory is a special symbol for all Mexican people who celebrate their rights of freedom and liberty, honoring those who fought, against the odds, for these principles.

WORSHIP

Opening Prayer

To begin the celebration, welcome participants and pray either of these prayers of liberty (or another from your own faith tradition).

> Great God: we thank you for this land so fair and free; for its worthy aims and charities. We are grateful for people who have come to our shores and crossed our borders, with customs and accents to enrich our lives. You have led us in the past, forgiven evil, and will lead us in time to come. Give us a voice to praise your goodness in this and every land, and a will to serve you, now and always; through Jesus Christ our Lord. *Amen.*[1]

> O eternal God, through whose mighty power our Fathers won their liberties of old; Grant, we pray, that we and all the people of this land may have grace to maintain these liberties in righteousness and peace; through Jesus Christ our Lord. *Amen.*[2]

---

1. "Prayer of Thanksgiving" adapted from *An American Prayer Book* by Christopher Webber (Harrisburg, PA: Morehouse Publishing, 2008), 36.

2. A prayer written in 1833 for an "American Independence Day Celebration" found in the 1928 Book of Common Prayer.

A MEXICAN FIESTA

Cinco de Mayo is the perfect event for a great Mexican fiesta theme party. While not a national holiday in Mexico (or the United States), it has morphed into a worldwide celebration of Mexican pride, culture, and heritage. Cinco de Mayo provides a fun opportunity to enjoy a fiesta with family and friends.

Materials

- decorations: piñatas, sombreros, Mexican flags, green and orange crepe streamers
- refreshments: plenty of food and drink (see some suggestions later in this chapter)
- CD player or MP3 player connected to speakers
- *optional:* mariachi band

Directions

1. Set your tables with bright, bold tablecloths in green and orange. Add a big sombrero, perhaps filled with a cactus plant. Use a serape as a table topper for additional color. Add more color with your paper goods and cutlery.
2. Hang an empty piñata for color and ambiance.
3. Don't forget to add Mexican-themed music. Download some great mariachi music, which always adds to any festivity.
4. To make the party informative as well as fun, choose other activities from this chapter.
5. Let people mix and mingle, and keep the atmosphere casual.

CRAFTS

Ojos de Dios (God's Eyes)

Many of us first made this craft at camp, but "God's eyes" (or *ojos de dios*) is thought to have originated with the Huichol Indians of western Mexico, where parents wove them as protective symbols for their children. The central eye was made when a child was born. Each year, a bit of yarn was added until the child turned five, at which point the *ojo* was complete. In Bolivia, "God's Eyes" were made and placed on an altar so that the gods could watch over the praying people and protect them.

Children five and up can do this with a little help from a parent holding the sticks steady; older kids can skip the glue and do it on their own.

Materials

- 2 twigs (or dowels or popsicle sticks), about 8" long, similar in thickness
- white glue
- 1 ball variegated yarn or balls of many colors of yarn
- child-safe scissors

Directions

1. At the center point of one twig, squirt a dab of glue then place the other twig in the glue, forming a cross. Let dry completely, about 2 hours. (Or hold tight as you begin to wind the yarn.)

2. Tie the loose end of the yarn to one twig, as close to the place where the twigs join as possible, leaving a 5" tail hanging from the knot.

3. Hold the cross in one hand, and with the other hand bring the yarn under one twig, around it, then over to the next one, under it, around it, and over to the next one, repeating that pattern all the way around the crossed sticks until you're happy with the size of the weaving.

4. You can mark the sticks with *1, 2, 3,* and *4.* The numbers will be covered up in the end, but this makes it easier for children to keep track of what they're doing. Wrap the wool once around 1, once around 2, once around 3, once around 4. Repeat until you're happy with the first layer of the eye.

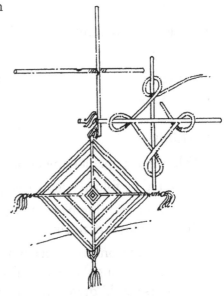

5. Snip the first color of yarn and tie on a second color. Continue on with the second color and then a third, fourth, and fifth as desired.

6. Trim the yarn, leaving a tail of about 10". Tie the two tails together and trim the ends.

Papel Cortado

Papel picado (punched paper) is a popular Mexican art form with roots in the country's ancient cultures. The Aztecs used the bark of wild mulberry and fig trees to make a rough paper called *amatl.* *Amatl* was used to make flags and banners to decorate temples, streets, and homes.

Today, professional craftsmen use awls, chisels, and blades to make intricate designs depicting flowers, birds, angels, crosses, skeletons, historic figures, and even words. They design the pattern on a piece of paper and then cut it out through as many as fifty sheets of tissue paper with their special tools. Sound complicated? Well, never fear . . . in its simplest form, *papel picado* is done as *papel cortado* (cut paper) and is made a lot like a paper snowflake. Toddlers and up will be proud to display their unique artwork!

Materials

- tissue paper (cut into pieces 8" x 10")
- scissors
- string
- clear tape

Directions

1. Fold tissue paper a number of times.
2. It should be folded edge-to-edge, not corner-to-corner.
3. For younger children, don't fold too many times or it will be difficult for them to cut.
4. Cut shapes from the paper, but don't cut off any corners (we want the rectangular shape of the tissue paper to remain). Note that nursery children and some preschoolers will need an older participant to do the cutting for them.
5. Unfold.
6. Edges may be straight, scalloped, zig-zagged, or fringed.
7. Fold the top ¼" of the *papel cortado* over a long piece of string and tape to make a pocket.
8. Add additional sheets in different colors to form a long, decorative streamer.

Milagros

Milagros are small, symbolic metal charms. The literal translation for *milagro* is *miracle*. Many Mexican people use milagros as tokens to represent something they would like help with or wish for. They accompany the milagro with a prayer. Traditional milagros include an ear of corn (for crops) and body parts (for healing that part of the body). Milagros are used in several cultures to ask or to give thanks for favors. Other cultures use milagros as good luck charms or jewelry. Some of the oldest charms have been found in Greece and Rome, where silver and gold were shaped into tiny master-pieces. The charms are usually shaped like an item or event. For instance, if you have a favorite pet, your milagro might be shaped like a dog or cat.

Shiny, bright Mexican milagros are a wonderful way to create your own "little miracles." What wishes do you want to come true? Think about something you would like help with, such as practicing music, improving your grades, or getting better at a sport. Think of a symbol for your wish, such as a piano, book, or sneaker. One fifth-grade class made milagros as reminders to pray for world peace, homeless people, and other concerns.

Materials

- *optional:* modeling clay or Crayola Model Magic®
- aluminum foil
- scissors
- colored pencils or gel markers
- construction paper
- string

Directions

1. Use clay or Crayola Model Magic® to create a small shape that has special meaning for you.
2. Cover the shape with aluminum foil and glue the ends of the foil in place if necessary. *Or* draw a shape of the symbol onto a piece of aluminum foil. Cut out the shape with scissors.
3. Make impressions in the surface of your symbol with colored pencils.
4. Cut a wish tag from paper. Write your wish on the tag with the colored pencils.
5. Poke a hole in the tag and in your symbol. Connect them with string.

Sun and Moon Myth Fan

Ready for hot days and sticky nights? Discover a fiery Mesoamerican myth while you cool off with a colorful fan. You might also do this activity before or after telling *The Legend of the Five Suns* on page 36.

Materials

- recycled file folder, poster board paper, or paper plate
- colored pencils, crayons, or markers
- scissors
- glue
- craft popsicle stick

Directions

1. Sketch a sun with pencils, crayons, or markers on a recycled file folder.
2. Experiment with different faces and try unusual shapes for the sun's rays. Color your sun with bright, warm colors such as yellow, orange, and red.
3. With scissors, cut around your sun.
4. Trace the outline on another file folder.
5. Sketch a crescent moon, or any other moon stage you wish, within the outline.
6. Add a face and other details such as stars and comets. Use cool colors, such as green, blue, and purple, to create a moody, cool moon. Cut out your moon.
7. Glue the sun and moon together, back to back.
8. For the fan handle, slide a craft stick between the two layers before the glue dries.
9. Air-dry your fan. For more fun, add patterns or designs to the fan handle. Stay cool!

STORYTELLING

The Battle of Puebla

You have several options to share the story of Cinco de Mayo: share the history given in the Introduction to this celebration or select a children's book with illustrations to read aloud in a story circle. Even adults will be engaged in a simple, colorful retelling of the story, as well as viewing the artwork. Check your local library or online. If your gathering is very large, split into smaller (mixed-age) groups and have each read their own storybook. Here are several possibilities:

- *Cinco de Mayo* by Mary Dodson Wade and Nanci R. Vargus
- *Celebrate Cinco de Mayo with the Mexican Hat Dance* by Alma F. Ada and F. Isabel Campoy
- *Viva Mexico! The Story of Benito Juarez and Cinco de Mayo* by Argentina Palacios and Alex Haley; illustrated by Howard Berelson
- *Cinco de Mouse-O!* by Judy Cox; illustrated by Jeffrey Ebbeler
- *Cinco de Mayo: Day of Mexican Pride* by Amanda Doering

Whatever method of storytelling you choose, consider including members of your congregation who are of Mexican descent to share the story of Cinco de Mayo. If possible, have your storyteller dress in traditional Mexican clothing, as might be seen at a Cinco de Mayo celebration. Include an explanation of the clothing and its history.

The Legend of the Five Suns

During Mexico's history, the sun has been an important symbol. Many different cultures have inhabited the *Estados Unidos Mexicanos* (United Mexican States). About twenty two hundred years ago, a temple was built in central Mexico. In time, this temple was used by many different groups of people. Later, people in the Aztec culture named it "Pyramid to the Sun."

The "Legend of the Five Suns" is from an Aztec tradition, but seemed to be widespread, with some variants through Mesoamerica (the land that is now Mexico). Read this story and then compare it to Genesis 1.

Materials

- 2–3 Mexican sun god images (An online search for "Mexican sun god" will yield several sites with appropriate—and slightly frightening—images.)

The Legend of the Five Suns

The Aztecs tell that the history of humanity has been through five eras, also called "Five Suns."

Ometecuhtli, the Divinity of all things and all beginnings, at the same time male and female, at the same time life and death, woke up once from his lethargy. He came to create his Four First Children. The First Children themselves had children, and so on. . . . The children and grandchildren of Ometecuhtli are the ones who created the world, the skies and humanity.

One of those gods, Quetzalcoatl first created something looking like a big half-sun. But he was so big that he couldn't move, and being only in half, he was not heating enough to create any life. So one of Quetzalcoatl's brothers, Tezcatlipoca laughed and kicked that useless sun back into chaos.

So at the beginning of the First Age, arose finally a whole sun, the Sun of the Jaguar (Ocelotl-Tonatiuh). He was created on a day "Four Jaguars." That Sun was under the will and rules of the God Tezcatlipoca. The gods also created a race of Giants. They were said to be very strong but monstrous. Also, there were at that time a lot of fierce creatures and animals. Tezcatlipoca's brother however, thought it was time for something else, that the reign of Tezcatlipoca had been enough and that those Giants were too monstrous. The Jaguar-Sun then fell from the sky, producing big damages on earth. The mountains collapsed, and obscurity came. Then all the fierce creatures, and particularly the jaguars with their night-vision, attacked the Giants and ate all of them. So ended the Sun of the Jaguar, the Sun of Earth.

The Second Sun arose on a day "Four Wind." He was the Wind-Sun (Ehecatl-Tonatiuh). Humans were created and they were surviving thanks to wild plants and hunt. Ehecatl was ruling on that Sun and on the creation. But again, one of the brothers, jealous of such reign, tried to put an end to it. Ehecatl had to flee, provoking hurricanes and tornados, wiping out all on his trail. Only some humans who could seek refuge in big trees and had changed themselves into monkeys survived. So ended the Sun of the Wind, The Sun of Air.

The Third Sun appeared on a day "Four Rain." He was named the Fire-Sun (Xiuh-Tonatiuh). Tlaloc was ruling in that era, and he provided abundant food to the people he created, making rain enough to compensate the burn of the Sun. Then came the time of jealousy again, because the people of that era did not respect the gods and were doing a lot of misdeeds. The other gods asked the powers of Fire to provoke a great cataclysm, and volcanoes erupted, and fire rain was falling from the sky. Only some humans, who had the idea to transform themselves into birds could flee quick enough before all got destroyed. So ended the Sun of Fire.

The Fourth Sun started on a day "Four Water." The Sun created then was the Water-Sun (Atl-Tonatiuh). The Goddess Chalchiuhtlicue was in charge of that Sun, and humans were given the aquatic plants and water-corn that she made for them. But again, time of misdeeds and jealousy came, and the Goddess let corruption seduce her. She had been convinced somehow that she had to put an end to that Age, and she began to unleash floods and torrential rains. Some humans could escape however, transformed into fishes for having been good swimmers for so long. Some also whispered that she let a couple of humans find safety on the biggest of the trees, and that in a hole there during the flood, they survived, keeping corn and the sacred fire alive. So ended the Sun of Water.

Then came the Time of the Fifth Sun. That Sun arose on a day "Four Movement." It is the Sun of our humanity, the Sun of the Aztecs. He has not ended yet. Some say he will end with earthquakes and explosions, but some say that he will maybe never end, because he is the synthesis of the four elements . . . that is if humanity can keep the balance. . . .

After telling the story, discuss

1. Why do you think the sun is so valuable to people living in Mexico? Think of the country's climate and geography. Compare this location to Norway or other northern countries. How do you think the sun is important to these people?

2. Show the pictures of the Mexican sun images. Continue the discussion. Most people think of sunny as meaning cheerful and happy. In Mexico, the sun has not always been portrayed as a happy face. Why do you think that is?

Remembering Victory

While the Battle of Puebla did not bring complete independence to Mexico, it did prove to the world that Mexico wanted the freedom to rule itself, and that it would fight courageously to obtain and preserve that freedom. It also revealed that a few people committed to a cause could triumph over a larger, better-equipped army of people less interested in the cause for which they were fighting. Finally, it showed that a country, which had been defeated time and time again, could, with perseverance, at last emerge victorious.

On a smaller scale, we each face conflicts each day. Whether competing against another team on the soccer field or struggling to understand a new rule in math, we are challenged. Sometimes we win immediately. Other times, we must try repeatedly before realizing victory.

Materials
- paper
- pens or pencils

Directions
1. Distribute paper and pens or pencils to participants.
2. Explain: Think back to the challenges you have faced in life—adjusting to life in a new city, learning how to read and write, making new friends, learning how to ride a bicycle without training wheels, earning money to buy something you really wanted and so forth.
3. Make a list of at least ten "victories" you can celebrate in your own life.
4. Allow 5–10 minutes for participants to write, then regather and invite volunteers to share items from their lists. You might also discuss:
   - How are our lists similar? different?
   - What did we learn about each other? about ourselves?
   - What helps us face challenges and not give up?
   - In what ways can we help each other—perhaps even this week—face a tough challenge?

MUSIC

Making Maracas

Amongst all the traditional styles of music in Mexico, the mariachi style is the one that is the most representative. It typifies how the world identifies Mexico, at least in terms of its music, folklore, and culture. Like all traditional music around the world, the mariachi was not invented by a single person, but instead is a result of a blend of religion, culture, and music. It is an intermingling of the indigenous culture with that of the Iberians and the other black slaves that followed them.

It is thought that the mariachi style of traditional Mexican music has its roots in religion. Christianity along with its religious music was brought over to Mexico by the Spanish conquerors. In fact, they used religious music to teach the natives about Christianity, and the instruments used to play the music were traditionally European. The natives of Mexico incorporated these new instruments, particularly the violin. The Spanish style of music flourished in the region, intermingling with the indigenous style of music until a blend of the two styles emerged.

Usually comprising three to five musicians, the orchestra of the mariachis is made up of guitars, violins, and trumpets, along with the traditional instruments of Mexico, the *guitarron* and the *vihuela*. The music is very lively and the musicians wear costumes that are elaborately embroidered and decorated, which comprise a large sombrero, tightly fitted pants, waist-length jackets, and boots.

You can join in the rhythm with these maracas!

Materials

- 9" paper plate
- markers or crayons
- handful of dried beans or rice
- stapler
- 5–6 strips of colored crepe paper or streamers

Directions

1. Decorate the outside (bottom) of the paper plate. Use bold designs and bright colors.
2. Fold the plate in half and put a handful of beans or rice inside.
3. Staple it shut.
4. Then staple the colored streamers to the curved side of the plate.
5. Now shake your maracas and make your own music!

Mexican Hymns of Praise

Materials

- *Wonder, Love, and Praise* (Church Publishing, 1997) or other songbooks

Directions

1. Sing together one or more Spanish songs of praise. These three are found in *Wonder, Love, and Praise:*

    - "Marcharemos en la Luz de Dios" ("We Are Marching in the Light of God") #787. This is a praise song, thanking God for freedom. The first verse is in English, the second in Zulu, and the third in Spanish.
    - "Muchos Resplandores" ("Many Are the Light Beams") #397. This is a song of being together in community—we are one in Christ.
    - "Unidos" ("Together") #796. Together, together, we gather in your name. Then we'll have in this world peace and love around us.

2. Use the maracas you may have created above to accompany the singing.

GAMES

Bandito Bingo

Once you get your fiesta going, play a few rounds of appropriately themed "Bandito Bingo." It is a ton of fun, with the grand prize winner being adorned as the Grande Bandito.

Bandito Bingo is played liked regular Bingo, but with a spin. Instead of pre-printed Bingo boards, make your own using words associated with Cinco de Mayo. You will need to make many cards, filling in the words in different order on each card. Note that you can also design and print cards from the template at *www.church publishing.org/faithfulcelebrations5*.

Materials

- copies of the Bandito Bingo Card Form (download a template at *www.churchpublishing.org/faithfulcelebrations5*)
- markers (pennies, Hershey's Kisses®, M&M's®, etc.)

Possible words

- fiesta
- amigo (male friend)
- amiga (female friend)
- guacamole
- mi casa (my house)
- torro (bull)
- piñata
- jalapeño
- tortilla
- Rio Grande (grand river)
- salsa
- adios (goodbye)
- hola (hello)
- señor (man)

- señorita (young woman)
- señora (woman)
- siesta (nap)
- familia (family)

Directions

1. To start, distribute the cards and spread the markers around the tables.
2. Invite a volunteer to be the *caller*. The caller randomly calls out words from the list. Players cover the words with a marker as they're called.
3. Play three rounds:

    - Round one can be a simple "five in a row."
    - Round 2 is to get two of the following: five across, down, or horizontal in a row. That winner can be crowned the "Pequeno (Small) Bandito."

4. The final game is to "cover the board," with the winner crowned the "Grande (Big) Bandito" of the fiesta with a big sombrero.

The catch: once you get "Bingo," you must sing, "Aye, Yae, Yae, Yae—I am an awesome bandito!"

RECIPES

Mexican Hot Chocolate

The people of Mexico have been drinking hot chocolate since the days of the Ancient Aztecs.

Ingredients

- 2 ounces unsweetened chocolate (2 one-ounce squares)
- ½ teaspoon vanilla
- 1 teaspoon ground cinnamon
- 4 tablespoons heavy cream
- 2 cups milk
- 2 egg yolks
- 2 tablespoons sugar
- *optional:* cinnamon sticks to stir

Supplies

- saucepan
- stove or hotplate
- hand beater or electric mixer
- large spoon for stirring
- spoons and mugs or hot beverage cups

Directions

1. In a saucepan, stir together chocolate, vanilla, cinnamon, and cream. Heat over *low* heat, stirring constantly until chocolate melts.
2. Slowly add the two cups of milk, while stirring. Mix well.
3. Let warm over *low* heat—*don't let it boil!*
4. Beat egg yolks and sugar until foamy. Slowly pour about ¼ of the chocolate mixture into the egg mixture, stirring constantly so the eggs heat *slowly* and you don't end up with scrambled eggs in your hot chocolate.

5. Pour the egg/chocolate mixture back into the saucepan. Beat until mixture is frothy.

6. Serve immediately with cinnamon sticks or spoons to stir with.

Makes 4 servings.

Polvorones (Mexican Sugar Cookies)

Ingredients

- 2 cups flour
- ¾ cup sugar
- ½ teaspoon cinnamon
- 1 cup butter or margarine

Supplies

- oven
- large mixing bowl
- electric mixer
- large spoon
- small spoons
- cookie sheets

Directions

1. Preheat oven to 300°F.
2. In a bowl, stir together flour, sugar, and cinnamon.
3. Cream the butter with a beater.
4. Add flour mixture ½ cup at a time to the butter while still beating until it is all incorporated.
5. Use a teaspoon to spoon out small pieces of dough and shape into a cookie.
6. Place on ungreased cookie sheets and bake 25 minutes.
7. *Optional:* Sprinkle warm cookies with sugar and cinnamon.

Makes 24 cookies.

Mexican Corn Bread

Maize, also known as corn, is a grass domesticated by indigenous peoples in Mexico in prehistoric times. The Aztecs and Mayans cultivated it in numerous varieties throughout central and southern Mexico, to cook or grind into flour. Over time, the crop spread throughout North America and then was brought to Europe by explorers in the fifteenth century.

Ingredients

- 1 cup yellow cornmeal
- 1 cup all purpose flour
- 1 tablespoon baking powder
- 2 tablespoons sugar
- 1 teaspoon ground cumin
- ½ teaspoon garlic powder
- ½ teaspoon chili powder
- ½ teaspoon salt
- ¼ cup canned chopped green chilies
- 1 cup milk
- ¼ cup butter, melted
- 1 egg

Supplies

- oven
- mixing bowl
- large spoon
- greased pan

Directions

1. Preheat oven to 425°F.

2. In a bowl, stir together cornmeal, flour, baking powder, sugar, cumin, garlic powder, chili powder, and salt.

3. Stir in chilies, milk, butter, and egg.

4. Pour into a greased 8" x 8" pan.

5. Bake for 20 minutes.

Makes 9 squares.

WORSHIP

Closing Litany

To conclude today's celebration, read responsively the litany below.[3] Recruit a volunteer to read the parts designated for the leader. Ask remaining participants to respond each time with "We thank you Lord" (for the first five responses) and "Hear our prayer" (for the remaining responses).

Leader: Heavenly Father, we give you thanks for the wonder of creation, for the gifts of human life, and for the blessing of human fellowship.

Participants: We thank you, Lord.

Leader: For Christ, your living Word, through whom we are taught the perfect way of life and dignity of service,

Participants: We thank you, Lord.

Leader: For your Spirit, who offers her gifts to us for the common good,

Participants: We thank you, Lord.

Leader: For the blessing of community in our nation, and for those who have used your gifts to strengthen and enrich its life,

Participants: We thank you, Lord.

Leader: For the Presidents of the United States and Mexico, and for all who serve as leaders in our lands,

Participants: We thank you, Lord.

Leader: Grant them, we pray, a vision of your will for your people; wisdom to fulfill their vocation of leadership in a nation of many races; strength and courage to carry out the duties of their calling; and the assurance of your presence, your power, and your love. Lord, in your mercy,

Participants: Hear our prayer.

Leader: We pray for all who are called to serve in times and places of crisis, in the face of racial and social tensions, at the borders of our countries. Lord, in your mercy,

---

3. Adapted from "Prayers for a National Holiday" #124 in *The Wideness of God's Mercy: Litanies to Enlarge Our Prayer*, edited by Jeffrey W. Rowthorn (New York: Church Publishing, 2007), 303.

Participants: Hear our prayer.

Leader: In the Church's proclamation of the Gospel, we ask for a clear message of your love and power. Lord, in your mercy,

Participants: Hear our prayer.

Leader: In the creation of laws, we pray for insight, integrity, and courage. In defense of our countries, we pray for justice and humility, fairness, and compassion. Lord, in your mercy,

Participants: Hear our prayer.

Leader: In industry and commerce, in trade and business, for mutual care and cooperation, and a concern for the good of all. Lord in your mercy,

Participants: Hear our prayer.

Leader: In art and music, theater and entertainment, sport and leisure, for recognition that all gifts come from you to give to one another. Lord, in your mercy,

Participants: Hear our prayer.

Leader: In education, in family and school and college, for a concern not only with information but also with maturity and fulfillment of life. Lord, in your mercy,

Participants: Hear our prayer.

Leader: And finally, in the service of those in need and sickness, anxiety and suffering, for a community that cares. Lord, in your mercy,

Participants: Hear our prayer. *Amen.*

Closing Prayer

O God, who created all peoples in your image, we thank you for the wonderful diversity of races and cultures in this world. Enrich our lives by ever-widening circles of fellowship, and show us your presence in those who differ most from us, until our knowledge of your love is made perfect in our love for all your children; through Jesus Christ our Lord. *Amen.*[4]

---

4. "For the Diversity of Races and Cultures" in the Book of Common Prayer, 840.

Chapter 3

MOTHER'S DAY

INTRODUCTION

We honor our mothers, being mindful of the fourth commandment, "Honor your father and your mother . . . that your days may be long" (Deuteronomy 5:16). This is also a day in which we honor women who have had an influence on our lives.

Why Celebrate Mother's Day?

The United States' observance of Mother's Day is held each year on the second Sunday in May. The holiday can be traced back to the Mother's Day Proclamation written by Julia Ward Howe in the aftermath of the American Civil War. It was a reflection of her pacifist reaction to the horrors of the war and her conviction that mothers had a rightful voice in the conduct of public affairs. There were other attempts to create a Mother's Day holiday in the ensuing years, but none succeeded beyond local observances.

The current holiday was created through the efforts of Anna Jarvis, continuing the work of her mother Ann Jarvis, who dreamed of creating a holiday to honor all mothers. With the help of Philadelphia department store magnate John Wanamaker, Jarvis persuaded President Woodrow Wilson to make it a national holiday in 1914.

Intentionally or not, the support of retail genius Wanamaker proved predictive, and Mother's Day soon became so commercially successful that many opposed it, including its founder Jarvis, who spent her inheritance and the rest of her life opposing it. Such opposition has done little to slow down the commercial juggernaut that Mother's Day has become. It is the most popular day of the year for dining out in a restaurant.

Mother's Day has also become the third most popular day for church attendance in the United States, behind only Christmas and Easter. There are no doubt many reasons for this phenomenon, beginning with the fact that the mother is statistically more likely to be the chief church attendance promoter in the family and the holiday in her honor gives her entreaties a particular irresistibility.

Past Celebrations of Mothers

But there is more to it than this. Women and mothers have been celebrated throughout the world's cultures since antiquity, although in ancient civilization more often as empresses or goddesses than as down-to-earth humans. It is only in relatively recent times that the role of the nurturing mother has come to be celebrated in her own right. In medieval Europe a tradition developed to relax the rigors of the Lenten fast on the fourth Sunday of Lent and for worshipers to return to the church of their baptism, or their Mother Church, for a celebration. In the 1600s this tradition was broadened in England to include recognition of actual mothers and became known as Mothering Sunday. There was a particularly humanitarian aspect of this observance in a society with strict laws of indentured servanthood, for it became customary for servants and other workers to be allowed time off to return to their homes and families for a family feast, with the mother as the honored guest.

The observance of Mothering Sunday waned in the early 1900s; however, its observance certainly points to the connection between the image of an actual mother and the "mothering church." Just as a mother gives food to her child, we go to church for spiritual food—*the sacraments*. Just as a mother consoles her child, the church through God's Word consoles us. Just as a mother dries her child's tears, in the church we find healing.

Planning

While the activities listed in this celebration are meant to be chosen for an intergenerational event, many of them can be done in advance with children to be able to give to mothers (theirs and others) at a celebration. You may wish to enlist the help of adults or youth to prepare a Mother's Day brunch.

Beyond the Celebration

If you're interested in extending the celebration beyond your church, home, or school, here are some suggestions:

- Remember on this day those mothers who may not be able to be with their children (and vice versa), for whatever reason. In your celebration at church be sure to include these folks in meaningful and loving ways.

- In our Baptism we are made a member of God's family. In a way we are adopted. We are given a new name—*Christian*—and we are sealed as Christ's own forever. In this larger "family" we have opportunities to honor *many* mothers and nurturers.

WORSHIP

Opening Prayer

Begin with the following prayer and/or choose a piece of scripture, literature, or poem to begin your celebration. See examples on pages 97, 58–59, 62, and 63–64.

> Gracious God, we give thanks today for mothers, our own and others we have known. Thank you for their gift of love to us, their care for us and for others. Help us to honor them as you would like us to do on this special day and every day. Give them strength to be good mothers and to love us as you love them. *Amen.*

CRAFTS

Mother's Day Flowers

Anna Jarvis (see page 50) began the tradition of giving a white carnation to mothers. This soon "blossomed" into a tradition of white flowers for your living mother, red flowers for your dead mother, and pink flowers for grandmothers, aunts, cousins, or friends who have had special influence on you. More flowers are given or sent on Mother's Day, as well as greeting cards, than any other day in the year. Invite participants to make Mother's Day flowers to give to others.

Materials

- pastel-colored tissue paper
- chenille stems (pipe cleaners)
- scissors
- ruler

Directions for making a single flower

1. Cut tissue paper into rectangles of desired size

2. Stack about 15 pieces of tissue paper. Use the same color or different colors. If you use fewer pieces of tissue paper, the flower will not be as full.

3. Accordion pleat the tissue paper, working from the long side.

4. Wind one end of the chenille stem around the middle of the accordion pleated tissue paper.

5. Trim the ends of each side to give the petals a unique look. Trimming the ends into a point (like a triangle) or a bump (like a half circle) will look very pretty.

6. Gently separate each layer, pulling upwards toward the middle of the flower. Do the second side.

7. Give your flower(s) to your mother or another special woman in your life.

Mother's Day Basket

Participants create Mother's Day baskets to give as gifts. If time allows, invite group members to make additional baskets for mothers and other women who may be alone on Mother's Day.

Materials

- paper plates, 1 per child
- stapler, glue, or glue sticks
- green construction paper cut into leaf and stem shapes
- colored cupcake papers for the flowers
- green chenille stems (green pipe cleaners)
- artificial shredded grass ("Easter grass" often found in Easter baskets)
- assorted materials for decorating, for example: sequins, stickers, etc.
- tape
- markers

Directions

1. Start with two paper plates.

2. Cut out a half circle from the edge of both plates, about a third of each plate. Make the shape and size of both cutouts the same.

3. Align the two plates front to front, lining up the cut-out areas, then staple or glue together the remaining outer edges to make a basket, leaving open the cut-out top.

4. Make flowers from cupcake papers. Stack several papers together, push a chenille stem through the center of the stacked papers, and fasten the stem on the back with tape. Gently spread apart the papers to make "petals" for the flower.

5. Create several flowers.

6. Tuck your flowers into your basket, filling in around the flower stems with the artificial grass.

7. Decorate the outside of the basket however you'd like.

8. Give to your mother or another special woman (grandmother, aunt, neighbor, family friend, coworker, teacher, etc.) in your life.

Mother's Day Banner

Invite all ages to get involved in creating this Mother's Day banner, assigning tasks as appropriate for various age levels.

Materials

- large sheet of butcher paper or newsprint (at least 6' long)
- markers
- magazines and newspapers
- scissors
- glue or glue sticks
- tape, tacks, or poster putty
- digital camera and photo printer (with photo paper)

Directions

1. Tape the sheet of butcher paper on the wall at a height where all can reach it.

2. Outline in large size the words *Happy Mother's Day.*

3. Invite everyone to decorate the mural with drawings, words, freshly taken and printed photos of mothers, images cut from magazines or newspapers—anything appropriate for Mother's Day.

4. Keep the banner on display for the entire community to enjoy in the coming weeks.

STORYTELLING AND BIBLE STUDY

Biblical Mothers Bible Study

Choose from the following scriptures, as appropriate for your group. Note that some stories will be appropriate for all ages; some may be challenging even for older participants. You could also consider reading a chosen story to youngest participants from a children's Bible, including one with illustrations.

Materials

- Bibles and children's Bibles
- pens or pencils
- paper

Directions

1. Select from the following scriptures:

   - Genesis 11–23: This is the story of Sarah.
   - Genesis 23–27: This is the story of Rebekah.
   - Exodus 2: This is the story of Moses' mother.
   - 1 Samuel 1–2: This is the story of Hannah, Samuel's mother, especially Hannah's prayer in 1 Samuel 2:1–11.
   - Luke 1:46–55: This is the Magnificat, the song sung by Mary, Jesus' mother, after learning she would give birth to God's Son. (You'll find many additional passages involving Mary throughout the Gospels; any of these could be used as well.)
   - Luke 1: This is the story of Elizabeth, mother of John the Baptist.
   - 2 Timothy 1: Here we learn of Lois, Timothy's grandmother.
   - 2 Timothy 1: And here we learn of Eunice, Timothy's mother.

2. Divide into smaller groups of 4–6 people each.
3. Provide each group a copy of the questions listed below.
4. Ask for a volunteer *within each small group* to read the chosen scripture passage(s) or story(ies), either in their own words,

from the Bible, or using a children's Bible appropriate for younger children.

5. Invite small groups to discuss the questions. Note that the first four are general and the last two refer to specific stories or passages.

Questions for each small group

- What did the mother in the story do that was very special?
- How did this mother feel?
- What do you think you would have done if you had been this mother?
- How did the children in these stories honor their mothers?
- In some of the readings we learn that the mother gave her child to someone else. How do you think that mother felt in giving away her child for a better life?
- If you chose to read the songs of both Hannah and Mary, compare and contrast the hymns each prayed. Do you think Mary knew Hannah's prayer and modeled her own on that one?

Mothers Reading Corner

Set up a reading corner for children in a carpeted spot with large pillows for sitting on. Children can read books quietly to themselves, or an adult or teen can read aloud to the group. The activity, "Book Study" (page 59), offers other suggested ways to use books. There are many wonderful picture books about mothers that your local library may have, including:

A Chair for My Mother by Vera B. Williams

Mama, Do You Love Me? by Barbara Joosse

Frances the Badger series by Russell Hoban

The Runaway Bunny by Margaret Wise Brown

Are You My Mother? by P. D. Eastman and Carlos Rivera

In God's Name by Sandy Eisenberg Sasso

I Wished for You: An Adoption Story by Marianne Richmond

Mommy, Mama, and Me by Lesléa Newman and Carol
Thompson

The Family Book by Todd Parr

Founding Mothers by Cokie Roberts and Diane Goode

In Our Mothers' House by Patricia Polacco

On Mother's Lap by Ann Herbert Scott

How to Babysit a Grandma by Jean Reagan

The Night Before Mother's Day by Natasha Wing

What Not to Give Your Mom on Mother's Day by Martha Seif
Simpson

A Book Study About Mothers

Materials

- one (or more) of the books listed above
- *optional:* Bible or children's Bible

Directions

1. Choose a book to read aloud to children from the list above.
   Make sure to hold the book open in front of you with the pictures facing out so everyone can follow along while you read.

2. After reading, discuss the following questions:

   - What does the mother do that makes her special?
   - Describe the love between mother and child.
   - In what ways is mothering different today than some years
     ago?
   - Do any of the mothers in the scripture readings or the
     books remind you of your mother? of you? of someone who
     was like a mother to you?

3. If you read either or both of the books *Mama Do You Love Me?*
   and *The Runaway Bunny*, discuss:

- Read aloud Psalm 139, then compare and contrast the psalm and the book.
- Read aloud Romans 8:35–39, then compare and contrast this reading and the book.
- With younger children, discuss:
  - Can you find the mother in this book?
  - What does the mother do that is very special for the child?
  - Does the child ask questions? Does the mother answer the child's questions?
  - Do *you* ask questions? From whom do you get answers?
  - Does the child in the story remind you of yourself?
  - Does the mother in the story remind you of your mother?

4. If you read the book *In God's Name*, you'll find many names are given for God to reflect God's many qualities. Discuss:

   - Is there one that speaks to you in a special way?
   - Are you offended by the less traditional names?
   - Do the different names help you understand the many natures of God?
   - Is there a name for God that you might use that is not in the book?

POETRY

Poems for Mother's Day

Invite participants to write cinquain poems for Mother's Day. You could also invite individuals to write poems of any other sort, including those that rhyme. However, providing a structure often makes this task easier, especially for participants lacking confidence in their "poetic skills."

Materials

- 4" x 6" notecards, several per participant
- pens, pencils, colored pencils, or markers
- stickers appropriate for Mother's Day
- *optional:* construction paper if cards are going to be made

Directions

1. Begin by explaining that cinquain poetry has five lines:
   - Line 1 is only one word (also the title of the poem).
   - Line 2 is two words that describe the title.
   - Line 3 is three words that tell of a related action.
   - Line 4 is four words that express a related feeling.
   - Line 5 is one word that recalls or echoes the title.

2. If you so desire, you may illustrate your poem.
3. You may also make a Mother's Day card, using your poem.

A Poem About Mothers

Materials

- copies of the poem "I Love You" by Carl Sandburg (quoted in *Elbert Hubbard's Scrap Book*, 1923), 1 per participant (you can also download this at *www.churchpublishing.org/faithful celebrations5*)

Directions

1. Distribute copies of the poem "I Love You" to participants.

2. Recruit two volunteer readers.

3. Ask the first reader to read the poem aloud as group members follow along.

4. Discuss the poem:

   - What does this poem say about a mother's love?
   - How is this like God's love?
   - What stories come to your mind when reading this poem?
   - What comes to your mind about your own mother when reading this poem?
   - What comes to your mind, as a mother, when you read this poem?

5. Ask a second reader to reread the poem aloud.

I Love You
by Carl Sandburg

I love you for what you are, but I love you yet more for what you are going to be.

I love you not so much for your realities as for your ideals. I pray for your desires that they may be great, rather than for your satisfactions, which may be so hazardously little.

A satisfied flower is one whose petals are about to fall. The most beautiful rose is one hardly more than a bud wherein the pangs and ecstasies of desire are working for a larger and finer growth.

Not always shall you be what you are now. You are going forward toward something great. I am on the way with you and therefore I love you.

PRAYER ACTIVITIES

Prayers

Choose from this selection of prayers to use when appropriate throughout today's celebration. Both *Women's Uncommon Prayers* and *She Who Prays, A Woman's Interfaith Prayer Book* have many wonderful prayers for and by women. Prayers for young children are better short in length and full of love. Don't be afraid to make up your own prayers for this age, or for any age for that matter.

> Merciful God, we remember Bilhah and Zilpah and their forgotten roles as the biological mothers to four of the tribes of Israel. We reject the practice of polygamy that pitted Rachel and Leah against each other and condemn the patriarchal system that enabled Rachel and Leah to give their respective maids to their husband Jacob, to produce more sons. Nevertheless we praise you that Bilhah and Zilpah were able to raise their sons, and that their sons were counted among the twelve tribes of Israel. We lift up all kinds of blended families, especially women who become surrogate mothers for economic reasons. We also give thanks for the women in our lives who are like mothers to us, regardless of how the relationship developed. *Amen.*[1]

> Eternal Spirit,
> Life-Giver, Pain-Bearer, Love-Maker
> Father and Mother of us all.
> Loving God, in whom is heaven:
> The hallowing of your name echo through the universe!
> The way of your justice be followed by the people of the world!
> Your heavenly will be done by all created beings!
> Your commonwealth of peace and freedom sustain our hope and come
>   on earth!
> With the bread we need for today, feed us.
> For the hurts we absorb from one another, forgive us.

---

1. "Bilhah, Genesis 30:6, and Zilpah, Genesis 30:11, and All Surrogate Mothers" in *She Who Prays*, 132.

In times of temptation and test, strengthen us.
From trials too severe to endure, spare us.
From the grip of all that is evil, free us.
For you reign in the glory of the power that is love,
Now and forever. *Amen.*[2]

O God of boundless love, make my love strong,
that I may perform with joy the duties of motherhood.
Help me persevere through times of fatigue and frustration.
Help me see the work of mothering as a sacrament,
bringing your love to life, making it tangible.
Help me become ever more aware of your countless blessings,
so to fill my heart with continual thanksgiving.
Dear Lord, I receive such joy from you.
Grant that I may find the time I need
to sit at the feet of Christ and listen,
to feel his closeness, to learn of his love for me.
Teach me to make all my actions prayer,
that busy or at rest I might always be near you.
Fill me with the quiet power of your Spirit,
so that through me, those I care for
may experience your most tender and merciful love.
Grant these my prayers for the sake of your Son Jesus Christ,
who loves us without measure. *Amen.*[3]

---

2. "A Mother's Prayer" by Karen A. Eshelman in *Women's Uncommon Prayers* (New York: Morehouse Publishing, 2000), 141.

3. "For Children" by Karen A. Eshelman in *Women's Uncommon Prayers*, 223.

CLOSING WORSHIP

A Litany for Mother's Day

A litany consists of petitions followed by a congregation's response. Feel free to add your own petitions as well.

Materials

- copies of the litany for participants

Advance preparation

1. Recruit volunteers of different genders and ages to take turns as leader throughout the litany.
2. Get copies of the litany to these volunteers in advance so they may practice ahead of time.

A Litany for Mothers

Leader: Let us give thanks to God for the many gifts we have been given.

People: We thank you Lord.

Leader: Today let us especially give thanks for our mothers, grandmothers, aunts, sisters, cousins, and friends who have been like mothers to us.

People: We thank you Lord.

Leader: For surrogate mothers who provide the gift of a child to those families who otherwise could not have children.

People: We thank you Lord.

Leader: For blended families who provide a loving home for the children and parents.

People: We thank you Lord.

Leader: For adoptive parents who welcome children into their home to love and care for them.

People: We thank you Lord.

Leader: We remember today those who are alone, who have no children, or whose children have moved away from home and can't be present today.

People: Good Lord, hear us.

Leader: We remember those mothers who suffer from famine, disease, and poverty and who see their children suffer.

People: Good Lord, hear us.

Leader: We remember today those who have lost a child or a mother.

People: Good Lord, hear us.

Leader: We remember today your Son's blessed mother, Mary. Help us to be kind and gentle as she was.

People: Good Lord, hear us.

All: These things we pray in the name of your Son, Jesus. *Amen.*

Chapter 4

MEMORIAL DAY

INTRODUCTION

Memorial Day is one of the most solemn days observed in the United States. On this day we remember those who gave their lives that we might have freedom. We may not agree with the notion of war or particular wars that have been fought, but these brave men and women were soldiers, fighting for their country, and so they deserve to be honored. As we honor those who have made sacrifices for our freedom, we can pray for justice and peace among all people.

Memorial Day is celebrated in the United States on the last Monday of May. The holiday was first known as Decoration Day and was held in honor of soldiers who had died in the U. S. Civil War. By the twentieth century, the holiday honored all U. S. soldiers killed in war. Originally the holiday included family visits to gravesites to clean up the area, place flowers, and say prayers for the deceased. Gradually this turned into family-reunion types of affairs and also focused on the beginning of summer.

It was popular to have a parade on Memorial Day featuring soldiers, veterans, and politicians. Clergy and famous soldiers gave speeches to commemorate the wars and rehash the horribleness of the enemy. Religion and nationalism joined together to make it possible for people to make sense of their history in terms of sacrifice and one nation under God. It didn't matter your denomination or, at that point, your country of origin. All became U.S. citizens on the battlefield.

The U. S. flag is usually flown at half-staff on Memorial Day, and it is a federal holiday. Flags are placed on the gravesites of veterans and those killed in battle. Parades are still popular, featuring military bands, and National Guardsmen and Guardswomen.

Why Connect Memorial Day with Our Faith?

We need to remember that the purpose of Memorial Day is to honor and to pray for those who have died, not the start of summer. Our freedom does not come cheaply. It has been bought with a dear price. We need to give thanks to our veterans for their tremendous sacrifice and that of their families.

Sadly today, there are people who vent their frustrations over war onto the returning warriors. Jesse Brown, secretary of Veteran Affairs, made the following observation, "To properly honor our dead, we must honor our living. The defenders of this Nation have fulfilled their obligations to us; it is now our duty to honor all of the obligations owed to them."[1]

A number of years ago, an editorial in *The Living Church* offered the following:

> While Memorial Day is not included in the church's calendar, it is a day [that] should be observed by all Christians. This holiday was created in 1868 to honor soldiers who were killed in the Civil War. In this century, those who died in subsequent wars also are remembered. Graves of veterans are marked with flags, and in many cases, Americans use the occasion to place flowers on the graves of loved ones.

> It is nearly impossible to observe Memorial Day without thinking about war. The tragedy of lives lost in such atrocities will never be forgotten, nor will the sacrifices of those who left homes, families and jobs to serve their country. If we meditate on such calamity, we may think about wars raging at present in various parts of the world and in our streets. We are anguished over the suffering, even death, some persons cause to others.[2]

---

1. "Observations on Memorial Day 1996" by Jesse Brown, Secretary of Veterans Affairs.
2. "Important Remembrance" editorial in *The Living Church* (May 26, 1996), 11.

Jesus gave us the solution to such conflicts when he said we should love each other. This answer may sound simplistic, but for Christians, they are words to live by. On this national holiday, may we remember those who have given their lives for this country, and may we be thankful for their sacrifices.

Poppies and Remembering

Memorial Day, *Decoration Day*, and *Remembrance Day* are names used around the world as countries honor those who gave their lives in war. In these countries, the day is usually a national holiday with parades, military bands, etc.

In the United Kingdom, Remembrance Day is one of the most solemn days of the year. The entire country observes a period of silence at 11:00 a.m. Red poppies are sold and people wear them on this day. In the United States, wreaths are laid at soldiers' tombs, especially at the Tomb of the Unknown Soldier.

The poppy is the enduring symbol of remembrance of the First World War. It is strongly linked with Armistice Day (November 11), but the poppy's origin as a popular symbol of remembrance lies in the landscapes of World War I. Poppies were a common sight, especially on the Western Front. They flourished in the soil churned up by the fighting and shelling. The flower provided Canadian doctor John McCrae with inspiration for his poem "In Flanders Fields," which he wrote while serving in Ypres in 1915.

Artificial poppies were first sold in Great Britain in 1921 to raise money to support ex-servicemen or the families of those who had died in conflict. In subsequent years, different charities began to sell poppies in different colors, each with their own meaning but all to commemorate the losses of war. White poppies, for example, symbolize peace without violence, and purple poppies are worn to honor animals killed in conflict.

Beyond the Celebration

Reach out to veterans' organizations and learn how you can support veterans in your community as well as those men and women who continue to serve in the military at home and abroad.

WORSHIP

Opening Prayer

O Judge of the nations, we remember before you with grateful hearts the men and women of our country who in the day of decision ventured much for the liberties we now enjoy. Grant that we may not rest until all the people of this land share the benefits of true freedom and gladly accept its disciplines. This we ask in the Name of Jesus Christ our Lord. *Amen.*[3]

---

3. "For Heroic Service" in the Book of Common Prayer, 839.

CRAFTS

Poppy Pictures (best for younger age levels)

Materials

- drawing paper, 1 sheet per child
- red stamp pads
- crayons
- several photos or drawings of red poppies
- wet wiping cloths (commercial cloths or damp rags)

Directions

1. Together, view the photos or drawings of the poppies. Observe how the red petals of the poppy fan out around a black center.
2. Distribute a sheet of drawing paper to each child. Make available the red stamp pads.
3. Demonstrate how to press your thumb onto the red stamp pad, then onto the paper to form a red petal. Continue to form petals in a circle, leaving a center area white. It may be easiest to keep rotating the paper as you add thumbprints.
4. Once children have completed one (or several) circles of petals, help them clean their thumbs using the wiping cloths.
5. Now invite children to draw stems, leaves, and the black center of the poppy.
6. For very young children, simply let them enjoy making red thumbprints all over their page. Watch out for red ink on clothing.

Crepe-Paper Poppies (best for older age levels)

Materials

- red crepe paper
- green chenille wires (pipe cleaners)
- black construction paper
- cellophane tape
- scissors

Directions

1. Cut the red crepe paper into 4" squares.
2. Gather 2 or 3 papers together, pleated like a fan.
3. Tightly wrap the end of a chenille stem around the center.
4. Cut and tape a circle of black construction paper over the stem where it is wrapped around the crepe paper, forming the black center of the poppy.
5. Carefully fluff out the paper to make flower petals and then round off the ends using scissors.

Memorial Day Placemats

Materials

- 11" x 14" sheets of Fun Foam® in red, white, and blue *or* large sheets of construction paper in red, white, and blue
- star stickers
- marker
- American flag (or a picture of one if a real flag isn't available)

Directions

1. Show the flag. Discuss why there are 13 stripes (13 original colonies) and 50 stars (number of U.S. states today) on the flag.
2. Cut the red foam or paper in 1" wide strips x 14" long.
3. Make a mark on the white foam or paper about 2" from each end. Cut slits in the white foam or paper 1" wide every 1". Then skip an inch, which will be a white stripe of the flag.
4. Now, weave your red strips in and out of the white foam or paper. End the red strip on the backside of the white foam or paper.
5. Decorate with star stickers.

STORYTELLING AND BIBLE STUDY

Reading Corner

Materials

- a variety of books (suggestions are listed below) from your local library or home collections
- pillows scattered on the floor for sitting upon

Book suggestions

- *The Wall* by Eve Bunting
- *Memorial Day* by Robin Nelson
- *Memorial Day* by Jacqueline S. Cotton
- *The Poppy Lady* by Barbara Elizabeth Walsh
- *America's White Table* by Margot Theis Raven
- *Wilfrid Gordon McDonald Partridge* by Mem Fox

Directions

1. Read any of the above books and discuss the following questions:

   - What is a memory?
   - Why is a memory important?
   - What can we do to make sure we remember?
   - What are we remembering on Memorial Day?
   - How can we help others remember?

Faith and Hope in God: Bible Study

Wisdom 3:1–9 is one of the scripture readings appointed for All Soul's Day (November 2) as well as for the Burial Office in the Book of Common Prayer. The messages align with our faith in God and hope that our deceased loved ones will be taken up into eternal life.

Materials

- Bibles
- poster board or flip cart
- markers
- tape, tacks, or poster putty

Directions

1. Distribute Bibles.
2. Turn together to Wisdom 3:1–9, helping younger participants as necessary.
3. Together rewrite Wisdom 3:1–9 (or portions of it) as a prayer, inviting group members to use contemporary language in place of the words found in their Bibles.
4. When the new prayer is completed, read it together (perhaps in unison), then discuss:

   - Are you familiar with this scripture? Where have you heard it read?
   - Does it remind you of other scriptures? Which ones and why?
   - Where is this celebration in the reading?

MUSIC

Patriotic Songs

Patriotic songs, and songs that recall and celebrate justice and freedom—and those who have given their lives for the cause of justice and freedom—are appropriate to incorporate throughout a celebration of Memorial Day. Suggestions are offered below, but feel free to supplement these with your own favorites. Consider asking veterans attending the celebration to identify their favorite patriotic songs; make a point of including these as well.

You might also play stirring, familiar patriotic tunes like marches by John Philip Sousa, "The Star-Spangled Banner" by Francis Scott Key, or "Over There" by George M. Cohan. Check your local library for recordings or visit iTunes or the Amazon.com MP3 store to purchase and download inexpensive MP3 versions of these songs.

Suggested songs

- "I Sing a Song of the Saints of God" (#293, *The Hymnal 1982*)
- "Eternal Father, Strong to Save" (#608, *The Hymnal 1982*)
- "My Country Tis of Thee" (#717, *The Hymnal 1982*)
- "Battle Hymn of the Republic" (#226, *Lift Every Voice and Sing II*)
- "Oh, Freedom!" (#225, *Lift Every Voice and Sing II*)
- "Free at Last" (#230, *Lift Every Voice and Sing II*)
- "A Song of Wisdom" (#905, *Wonder, Love, and Praise*)
- "Holy God, You Raise Up Prophets" (#792 in *Wonder, Love, and Praise*)

POETRY

Memorial Day Poems

Materials

- copies of the "Memorial Day Poems" found below and on page 77, 1 per participant
- *optional:* poster board or flip chart with markers

Directions

1. Read through each of the two poems.
2. Within small groups (of mixed ages), discuss the following questions, which you may want to write out in large letters on poster board or a flip chart for all groups to see.
   - What do these two poems share in common?
   - Why is the soldier in "The Soldier's Faith" "content"?
   - What symbol does the "In Flanders Fields" poet use? Why?
3. *optional:* Can you tie these poems into the Wisdom reading on page 73?

The Soldier's Faith

author unknown

And when the wind in the tree-tops roared,
The soldier asked from the deep dark grave:
"Did the banner flutter then?"
"Not so, my hero," the wind replied.
"The fight is done, but the banner won,
Thy comrades of old have borne it hence,
Have borne it in triumph hence."
Then the soldier spake from the deep dark grave:
"I am content."

Then he heareth the lovers laughing pass,
and the soldier asks once more:
"Are these not the voices of them that love,
That love—and remember me?"

"Not so, my hero," the lovers say,
"We are those that remember not;
For the spring has come and the earth has smiled,
And the dead must be forgot."
Then the soldier spake from the deep dark grave:
"I am content."

Historical Note: This poem was quoted by Oliver Wendell Holmes
Jr. in a Memorial Day speech at Harvard in 1895.

In Flanders Fields
Dr. John McCrae

In Flanders fields the poppies blow
between the crosses, row on row,
that mark our place; and in the sky
the larks, still bravely singing, fly
scarce heard amid the guns below.

We are the Dead. Short days ago
we lived, felt dawn, saw sunset glow,
loved and were loved, and now we lie,
in Flanders fields.

Take up our quarrel with the foe:
to you from failing hands we throw
the torch; be yours to hold it high.
If ye break faith with us who die
we shall not sleep, though poppies grow
in Flanders fields.

Historical Note: This poem was written by a Canadian soldier
during World War I and is one of the most-quoted and well-
known poems of the war. Dr. John McCrae wrote the poem after
the death of one of his good friends at the Battle of Ypres. He was
dissatisfied with the poem and threw it away. Some of his fellow
soldiers retrieved it. The red poppy became an international symbol for the day, and red poppies are sold by soldiers on Remembrance Day and Memorial Day.

FAITH IN ACTION

Care Boxes

Invite all participants to help prepare care boxes for those serving in the military.

Materials

- donated items to be packed and shipped to deployed family members (see Advance Preparation, below)
- list of addresses for deployed church members (and perhaps those beyond your own faith-community—neighbors, coworkers, etc.; see Advance Preparation, below)
- packing boxes and packing tape
- marker
- note cards and envelopes
- pens or pencils
- drawing paper and crayons/colored markers

Advance preparation

1. Check with your local recruiting office or online at www.the-soldiersfamily.com for suggestions of items to include in care boxes for military personnel.
2. Put out the invitation (via church newsletter, church e-mail list, announcement during worship, and/or church website) for needed items. Invite participants to bring these to the celebration.

Directions

1. Spend time during the celebration sorting items and packing the boxes.
2. Invite children to draw pictures to include in the boxes. Invite older children, youth, and adults to write personal notes to include as well.
3. Seal, address the packages, and arrange for their shipping.

CELEBRATION BBQ

Materials

- list of those in your church who have served and are serving in the armed forces
- all the supplies necessary for a typical summer BBQ
- memorabilia brought by guests who have served and are serving in the armed forces
- photo display of veterans who have died
- hymnals
- *optional:* musical instruments and people to play them

Advance preparation

1. Contact those on the list of vets and armed service members provided by your church. Invite them to the celebration, asking them to be prepared to share stories, photos, prayers, hymns, or scriptures that kept them going during difficult times in the service.
2. Prepare the display of photos of those who died while serving in the military.
3. Plan a "Hymn Sing" and recruit accompanists.

Directions

1. Celebrate together with good food, fellowship, games, and a time of quiet reverence to honor those who have served and are serving in the military, especially remembering those who gave their lives for our freedom. (This may be a good time to incorporate one or more of the prayers found on page 70 or 80.)
2. Be sure to use the Memorial Day placemats if you created them earlier in the session, as well as to wear the red poppies some members may have made. Poppies could also be used as table decorations.

WORSHIP

Closing Prayers

Choose from this selection of prayers or those on page 70 to conclude your celebration.

> Almighty God, we commend to your gracious care and keeping all the men and women of our armed forces at home and abroad. Defend them day by day with your heavenly grace; strengthen them in their trials and temptations; give them courage to face the perils which beset them; and grant them a sense of your abiding presence wherever they may be; through Jesus Christ our Lord. *Amen.*[4]

> O God, you have bound us together in a common life. Help us, in the midst of our struggles for justice and truth, to confront one another without hatred or bitterness, and to work together with mutual forbearance and respect; through Jesus Christ our Lord. *Amen.*[5]

---

4. "For Those in the Armed Forces of Our Country" in the Book of Common Prayer, 823.

5. "In Times of Conflict" in the Book of Common Prayer, 824.

Chapter 5

FATHER'S DAY

INTRODUCTION

On this day on which we honor our fathers, we are mindful of the fourth commandment, "Honor your father and your mother . . . that your days may be long" (Deuteronomy 6:16). In a country in which one quarter of all children live without a father, we also honor those who live in nontraditional families. This is also a day in which we honor men who have had influence on our lives.

The Origins of Father's Day

Father's Day is the annual holiday honoring fathers and celebrating fatherhood. Movements for its creation began in the early twentieth century at the same time as a similar push for Mother's Day was taking place. A bill was introduced in Congress is 1913 proposing that Father's Day become a national holiday. Although President Woodrow Wilson went to Spokane, Washington to speak at a Father's Day celebration, Congress was not in favor of designating the day a holiday because they were afraid it would become too commercialized.

In 1957, Maine Senator Margaret Chase Smith made another proposal for the creation of Father's Day, citing the creation of Mother's Day in 1914 and accusing Congress of neglecting fathers for over forty years. Finally, in 1972, Richard Nixon signed into law the proclamation to designate the third Sunday in June as Father's Day.

The impetus for the creation of Father's Day, like that for Mother's Day, originated at a time in which the vast preponderance of homes consisted of a mother and father and their children. That is no longer the case. Almost one-fourth of American children under the age of 18 live in a home with a single mother.

According to the 2013 U.S. census:[1]

- 66 percent of children, ages 0–17, lived with two married parents (compared with 81 percent in 1970);
- 7 percent of children lived with two unmarried, co-habiting parents (compared with 3 percent in 2003);
- 25 percent of children lived only with their mothers;
- 6 percent of children lived only with their fathers;
- 4 percent of children lived with neither their mother nor their father; and
- of children living with a grandparent, 20 percent did not have a parent present.

These numbers are part of a trend that began in the mid-twentieth century and show no signs of slowing down. Many people in our country feel that there is a war on the family at work in our society—a conscious effort on the part of some to promote a lifestyle free from the constraints and responsibilities that a committed marriage requires. It is much more likely that what we are seeing is the result of the interaction of a vast number of cultural, economic, and demographic factors. While it is unlikely that the trends can be reversed, there are certainly things that we as Christians can do to address some of the underlying factors that work against the creation and maintenance of stable families.

The reality is that there are and will be a large number of "nontraditional" family configurations in our society. Some families have two dads or two moms. And single parents (adoptive or by birth) provide stable environments for the raising of children successfully.

---

1. *www.census.gov/newsroom/press-releases/2013/cb13-199.html* (accessed October 1, 2018)

Instead of focusing on the once "traditional" family unit, we should focus our efforts on spreading the message of God's love for us to *all* families, whatever they may look like. It is great to have a mom and dad, but you can also have a wonderful family with just a mom or a dad, or with a grandparent or with two moms or two dads. And all of these families will be blessed and strengthened if they are a part of a loving faith community.

Beyond the Celebration

If you're interested in extending the celebration beyond your church or local community, here are some suggestions:

- Remember on this day those fathers who may not be able to be with their children, for whatever reason. In your celebration be sure to include these folks in meaningful and loving ways.
- In our Baptism we are made a member of God's family. In a way we are adopted. We are given a new name—*Christian*—and we are sealed as Christ's own forever. In this larger "family" we have opportunities to honor *many* fathers and nurturers.

WORSHIP

Opening Prayer

Choose one or more of these prayers to begin your celebration.

> Gracious God, we give thanks today for fathers, grandfathers, uncles, brothers, godfathers—our own and others we have known. Thank you for their gift of love to us, their care for us and others. Help us to honor them as you would like us to do on this special day and every day. Give them strength to be good fathers and to love us as you love them. *Amen.*

> Most gracious God, we thank you for fathers, grandfathers, uncles, and other men who have had an impact on our lives. Please help us to honor them, their memories, their gifts to us. *Amen.*

> Almighty God, heavenly Father, you have blessed us with the joy and care of children: Give all fathers calm strength and patient wisdom as parents, that they may teach them to love whatever is just and true and good, following the example of our Savior Jesus Christ. *Amen.*[2]

---

2. Adapted from "For the Care of Children" in the Book of Common Prayer, 829.

CRAFTS

Father's Day Collages

Using photographs and clippings from magazines, participants can create collages to honor their fathers or other men who have had an impact on their lives.

Materials

- 11" x 17" pieces of poster board, 1 per participant
- glue or glue sticks
- magazines
- photos of participants' fathers, grandfathers, uncles, etc. (see Advance Preparation, below)
- markers
- scissors
- a variety of additional decorative items, like stickers, ribbon, gummed stars, construction paper, foil scraps, fabric scraps, etc.

Advance preparation

- Let parents know beforehand that they should bring photos of fathers, grandfathers, uncles, and other significant men in their children's lives (like teachers, neighbors, coaches, etc.) to the celebration. Alert them to the fact that these photos will be used in a collage and so may be cut and glued into place.

Directions

1. Invite each child to create a collage celebrating their father (or other influential men in their lives). If dads are present, do this activity together, with the dad sharing stories about the images.
2. Distribute a sheet of poster board to each child (and their parent or family unit).
3. Use the photos brought for each child/family as well as pictures found in the magazines, which can be cut or torn out.
4. Arrange the pictures on the poster board, then glue them into place.

5. Use markers and any other items to decorate the poster or describe the images.

6. If this is being made as a gift, each participant can give their completed collage to their father (or grandfather or another father figure) for Father's Day.

7. *Note*: Nursery- and preschool-age children will need help with all the steps in this project; pair up these younger participants with their fathers, mothers, or older siblings.

Alternative activities

- Invite fathers to create similar collages celebrating their relationship with their children.

- Invite family units to create collages of the favorite things they enjoy doing together.

Picture Frames

A fun gift to make and give.

Materials

- 4" x 6" photo of each person attending the celebration (see Advance Preparation, below)
- Fun Foam® pictures frames with 4" x 6" openings, 1 per participant (or their equivalent) *or* colored poster board that could be cut to create frames
- rulers
- assorted decorations such as: sequins, gummed stars, stickers, rickrack, ribbon, additional Fun Foam® shapes (or their equivalent)
- glue or glue sticks
- scissors
- colored construction paper, colored foil, other decorative papers
- brown paper lunch bags

- markers
- photo tape (like cellophane tape, but designed without acid for use with photos; available at craft and office supply stores)
- digital camera(s) and photo printers with 4" x 6" photo paper

Advance preparation

- Invite participants to bring 4" x 6" photos of themselves to the celebration.
- Arrange for several participants to bring their digital cameras and at least one photo printer with printer paper.

Directions

1. Distribute a photo frame to each participant *or* invite each participant to create a photo frame by cutting a rectangle of poster board (larger than 4" x 6"), then cutting another rectangle out of the center of this rectangle to be slightly smaller that 4" x 6".
2. If necessary, take and print photos of participants who were unable to bring photos.
3. Tape the photo to the back of a picture frame so the image shows through on the front.
4. Decorate the frame using the available materials.
5. Somewhere on the frame (front or back), write "To my _____." (This will be the person to whom you will give your framed photo, for example, your father or grandfather.)
6. "Wrap" your framed photo in the brown paper lunch bags.
7. Give this photo to the person you've chosen as the recipient.

Father's Day Aprons

Many fathers like to cook, both indoors and out. Surprise them with special aprons designed just for them in honor of their special holiday.

Materials

- white aprons, 1 per participant (inexpensive white aprons can be purchased at restaurant supply stores or from *www.oriental trading.com/api/search?Ntt=aprons*)
- disposable aluminum pie pans, heavy-duty (coated) paper plates, or disposable foam plates
- acrylic paint
- fabric marker pens

Directions

1. Give each participant a white apron. (For the families present, have each family join together to create a single apron.)
2. Pour each color of paint into its own disposable pie pan or paper plate.
3. Demonstrate how to put your hand—palm down—in the paint. Then carefully place your hand on the apron.
4. Write your name by your handprint.
5. Write *Happy Father's Day* with a fabric marker on the apron.
6. Invite group members to follow this same process to create aprons for their fathers (or other significant "father figures").
7. Encourage group members to give their hand-decorated aprons to their fathers (or other significant "father figures").

Optional activity

- Decorate a grocery bag with father pictures (cut from magazines), colored streamers, and stickers, and place nonperishable items for a Father's Day cookout in the bag. Place the apron on top. Close up and give to your father on Father's Day.

STORYTELLING AND BIBLE STUDY

Father's Day Panel Discussion

Invite fathers of all ages and backgrounds to share their stories.

Advance preparation

- Recruit a small group of diverse fathers representing different ages and ethnicities for a panel discussion during the celebration.
- Ask these volunteers to be prepared to talk about how it was (or is) to raise children in our unsteady, insecure world.

Preparation

- Set up chairs for each panelist so they face an audience

Directions

1. Seat panel members in front of the group.
2. Invite each panel member to talk briefly about their experience of fatherhood, as prompted before the celebration.
3. Invite additional questions from the group; here are some suggested questions to help you get started:
   - What advice would you give to a new father?
   - What additional life advice would you give to your children *now?*
   - How is/was your faith community (this one or another) a help to them? a hindrance?
   - What is your most sacred memory of parenting?

Biblical Fathers Bible Study

Choose several of the following scriptures, as appropriate for your group. You could also consider reading a chosen story to younger participants from a children's Bible, including one with illustrations.

In the case of the stories of Abraham, Jacob, Joseph, and Moses—all of which are long and complicated—you might have someone prepare a summary of these stories, if you choose one or more of them; such stories may also be better covered by a children's storybook based on the character's life, which will cover the highlights and be accessible for all ages.

Materials
- Bibles
- pens or pencils
- questions for small groups
- *optional:* children's Bibles or Bible storybooks

Directions
1. Provide Bibles to all participants.
2. Divide into smaller groups of 4–6 people each.
3. Provide each group a copy of the questions listed below.
4. Ask for a volunteer *within each small group* to read the chosen scripture passage(s) or story(ies), either in their own words, from the Bible, or using a children's Bible appropriate for younger children. In the case of the stories of Abraham, Jacob, Joseph, and Moses, have someone either summarize their stories or read abbreviated versions from a children's Bible or children's storybook.
5. Invite small groups to discuss the questions.

Select from the following scriptures
- Exodus 20:12 (the fourth Commandment)
- Abraham (Genesis 20–23)
- Jacob (Genesis 29–49)
- Joseph (Genesis 42–50)
- Moses (Exodus 2–20)
- Psalm 103:13

- Ephesians 6:4
- Psalm 139
- Romans 8:35–39

Questions for discussion
- What does this passage say about fathers?
- Would you have wanted this person to be your father?
- What is the most outstanding thing this father did?
- Have you ever been in such a situation?
- What does this scripture say to you as a father?
- What does this scripture say to you about your own father?

A Reading Corner with Dad

Create an area for dads (or moms or others) to read books with their children. Small groups can gather together with a book or the whole group can share a storybook together and talk about it after reading.

Materials
- one or more books (chosen from the list below)
- *optional:* Bible
- comfy seating on the floor with pillows

Directions
1. Choose one of the books listed below from your local, school, or church library or from someone's personal library. Most of the books listed are appropriate for children grades 3–5 and older. Some of the books are appropriate for older youth and for adults as well.
2. With older participants, discuss the following questions:
   - To what extent did (or does) your father play a significant role in your life that helped (helps) you become a well-grounded person? How has he influenced your outlook on life?

- If you are a father, what could you do as a father to help your child through a crisis? to share good times? to be a good example?
- Is there another "father figure" in your life who helped you through a difficult time or shared joyful times with you?

3. If you read *Papa, Do You Love Me?*, also read aloud Psalm 139 and/or Romans 8. Compare and contrast the message of the book and either (or both) of the scripture readings. What does this tell us about being a father?

Possible book choices

- *Papa, Do You Love Me?* by Barbara Joosse
- *Ramona and Her Father* by Beverly Cleary
- *Daddy, Papa, and Me* by Lesléa Newman and Carol Thompson
- *Dad By My Side* by Soosh
- *Because I'm Your Dad* by Ahmet Zappa
- *Made for Me* by Zack Bush

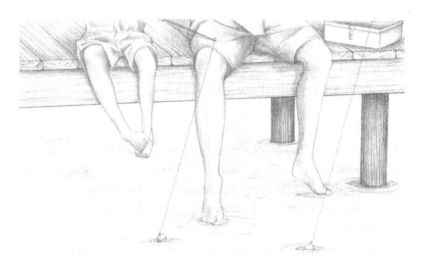

GAMES

Father's Day offers a perfect opportunity for outdoor fun. Here are three hilarious relay races you can try. All ages can join in for these memorable fitness-boosting, laughter-inducing games.

Dress Like Dad Relay

This two-team relay race works especially well when two families compete.

Supplies

- Two good-sized laundry baskets
- Two full outfits that dads like to wear (Each family can bring an outfit that their dad likes to wear that he doesn't mind getting a little rumpled.) You can make it a casual outfit—tee shirt, sweatpants, athletic socks, shoes, sweatshirt—or a formal one with button shirt, jacket, tie, pants, and so on. Just be sure that each basket has similar types of clothing, with at least 4–5 pieces.
- *optional:* hula hoop

Directions

1. For the race, select one person who will end up dressed "just like Dad." This could be anyone—but it's especially fun to pick a kid. Have that person stand just to the side behind the start line, perhaps sitting in a chair or standing in a hula hoop circle.
2. Appoint a referee to start the race and call the finish. Then each team member will take turns running a relay.
3. To play, a runner must race to the laundry basket, select one item of Dad's clothing, put it on, and then run back to the finish line with it (yes, shoes and pants tend to make for some especially good laughs). While the next racer heads off, the team must quickly take this item off the person and put it on the person selected to be "Dad."
4. The first team to dress "Dad" completely wins the round!

Golf Relay Race

Does dad love to hit the links in nice weather? Here's a "golf" relay race that the whole family can play.

Supplies

- Cones or a rope
- Badminton racquets—one per team (A lightweight child's tennis racquet will also do, or if you're really stumped, you can try a thick whiffle ball bat.)
- Small beach ball

Directions

1. Give each team one badminton racquet.
2. Then give each team a small (5–6") inflated beach ball.
3. Use the same size course as for "Dress Like Dad Relay," but this time leave your laundry basket upside down to mark the far end.
4. To play, each team sends one racer at a time, in a relay. Keeping the beach ball no higher than your knees, bat it across the field, around the basket, and back again. First team to return all players, plus beach ball, wins the round!

Egg Spoon Races

If you're very bold, you can use plain eggs right from the carton. Most folks find, however, that hard-boiled eggs are a safer solution!

Supplies

- 8 eggs per team, hard-boiled or right from the carton
- one large cooking spoon per team
- one shallow bowl per team

Directions

1. Gather one large cooking spoon and eight eggs per team (okay, a couple of backups might be a good idea).

2. Use a non-toxic marker to mark your eggs with letters, one letter per egg, to spell D-A-D R-O-C-K-S.

3. Use the upended laundry baskets to mark the end of your course, but this time place the eggs in a shallow bowl on top. Each racer must run to the basket, scoop an egg with the spoon only (no hands!), and then, holding the spoon in front, race back to the starting line.

4. Players can pick up letters in any order, but by the end, the first team that can spell "Dad Rocks" completely is the winner!

Note: Leftover eggs can still be used for cooking, and eating, too, if they're returned to a refrigerator promptly.

FAITH IN ACTION

Gift Bags

While we might not know if they are fathers or not, many men who live in homeless shelters are fathers, uncles, and grandfathers. Contact your local shelter or food pantry and find out what personal needs the men might have. Put out a call for participants to bring such items to your celebration, and take time to put together gift bags to be delivered to your local agency.

Supplies

- large plastic zipper bags for holding your collected supplies

Types of items to collect

- *toiletries:* deodorant, toothpaste, toothbrushes, nail files, shampoo, sunscreen, lotion, combs
- *clothing:* new socks, handkerchiefs, underwear
- small, collapsible umbrellas
- $10 gift cards to local coffee shops

RECIPES

Brunch Buffet

Dads are breakfast people. Moms might want breakfast in bed for their day, but dads just want to make sure that there is breakfast—and lots of it. Pancakes are always a popular choice, but which kind to serve? Plain? Blueberry? Banana and chocolate chip? Pecan? Why not all of them? And it doesn't have to be for breakfast—why not brunch or evening dinner?

Take one pancake or pizza recipe (or use both, such as noted below) and show how you can create a pancake/pizza buffet of toppings that can be mixed and "cooked to order" during a leisurely meal for Dad. Older kids can cook while younger kids can serve. Other adults can supervise. Simply add other items to your buffet—don't forget the bacon and coffee!

Pancakes

Ingredients

- 2 cups all-purpose flour
- 1 tablespoon baking powder
- ½ teaspoon baking soda
- ½ teaspoon kosher salt
- 2 eggs
- ¼ cup sugar
- 1¾ cup buttermilk
- ¼ cup whole milk
- ½ stick unsalted butter (4 tablespoons), melted and cooled

Pancake filling ideas

- 1 cup chocolate chips
- 1 cup candied pecans, chopped
- 2 bananas, sliced thinly
- 1 cup fresh blueberries
- 1 cup fresh raspberries

Pancake topping ideas

- Strawberry sauce
- Whipped cream
- Maple syrup
- More chocolate chips!

Supplies

- griddles for the stove or electric frying pans
- spatulas
- bowls for mixing batter
- bowls for placing ingredients for toppings

Directions

1. In a large bowl sift together the flour, baking powder, baking soda, and salt, and set aside.
2. Whisk together the eggs, sugar, buttermilk, milk, and melted butter. Fold the dry ingredients into the wet ingredients, taking care to not overmix. (The batter will have some lumps.)
3. Using a ladle, pour about ½ cup of batter onto a heated nonstick skillet. Sprinkle the top with the filling of your choice. Once the batter begins to bubble (about 2–3 minutes), flip the pancake and cook the other side for about the same amount of time.
4. Then let each person top their custom pancakes with any of the toppings.

Breakfast Pizza

Dads and kids can work together to come up with fantastical, imaginative breakfast pizza ideas. Get creative to develop weird, wacky, and tasty types of this food favorite.

Ingredients

- frozen/refrigerated pre-made pizza dough
- flour

- For toppings, choose from:
  - Cheese (any)
  - Bacon
  - Vegetables: tomatoes, peppers, celery, asparagus, etc.
  - Peanut butter or other nut spread
  - Fruit: bananas, strawberries, blueberries, sliced pears, sliced apples, etc.
  - Anything else your little one can think up!

Supplies
- rolling pin
- pizza stone or pan
- oven

Directions
1. Mold the dough into a sphere. On a floured work surface, roll the dough out into a traditional pizza circle shape.
2. Preheat the oven to 350°F or follow the directions on the pre-made dough package. This step should only be done by an adult.
3. Come up with an imaginative breakfast pizza menu. Try a cheese and sliced veggie pie, peanut butter pizza (add the peanut butter to a cooked crust, do not cook the peanut butter), or a breakfast bacon treat.
4. Bake the pizza for approximately 20 minutes or until fully cooked and golden brown.

WORSHIP

Conclude your celebration with this litany.

Leader: Let us give thanks to God for the many gifts we have been given.

People: We thank you Lord.

Leader: Today, let us especially give thanks for our fathers, grandfathers, uncles, cousins, and friends who have been like fathers to us.

People: We thank you Lord.

Leader: For surrogate fathers who provide the gift of a child to those families who otherwise could not have children,

People: We thank you Lord.

Leader: For blended families who provide a loving home for the children and parents,

People: We thank you Lord.

Leader: For adoptive parents who welcome children into their home to love and care for them,

People: We thank you Lord.

Leader: We remember today those who are alone, who have no children, or whose children have moved away from home and can't be present today.

People: Good Lord, hear us.

Leader: We remember today those who have lost a child or a father.

People: Good Lord, hear us.

Leader: We remember today your Son's blessed earthly father, Joseph. Help us to be kind and gentle as he was.

People: Good Lord, hear us.

All: These things we pray in the name of your Son, Jesus. *Amen.*

Chapter 6

SUMMER SOLSTICE

INTRODUCTION

Humans have always sought to understand the natural phenomena that impact their lives. Conflicts between faith and science have come about as science offers explanations that previously were understood as the work of God. Our God is big enough to handle this.

Since the dawn of civilization, the earth's people have attempted to make sense of the world around them. They knew that seasons of sun and rain caused the crops to grow. They saw the unpredictability of volcanoes and floods that killed and destroyed. They began to notice celestial rhythms that gave order and predictability to life. They looked at rainbows and other natural wonders that seemed to produce nothing but awe and wonder in their beholders.

It is natural that all cultures have their own myths to explain the phenomena of nature and have developed religious observances, feasts, sacrifices, and other means of marking these phenomena. Many cultures throughout the world placed particular emphasis on what they viewed as the annual journey of the sun through the sky. It was important because it seemed it gave order to the annual seasons and the predictability that made their lives possible.

The summer solstice, which takes place on June 20 in the Northern Hemisphere, is the day in which the sun reaches its most northern point in the sky and produces the longest daylight of the year. The summer solstice occurs when Earth's axis or pole is tilted toward the sun.

Planet Earth is tilted at about 23.5 degrees. This means that at different times of the year, either the northern or the southern hemisphere is closer to the sun. When the northern hemisphere is tilted towards the sun, the United States and Canada experience the longer warmer days of summer, while those in the southern hemisphere experience the shorter colder days of winter and vice versa. The day was deemed by ancient peoples as a special event, with supernatural implications for fertility in both humans and livestock herds, and for favorable growing conditions for the summer season.

Celebrating the Solstice Today

Modern celebrations of the summer solstice are often linked to the prehistoric structure in England known as Stonehenge. Although differing theories exist as to its purpose, there is agreement that its celestial observatory function included a spectacular focus on the rising sun at the summer solstice, and it must have certainly been the site of annual observances of the event. In many places throughout the world, especially in Northern Europe, the summer solstice is still celebrated with festivals and bonfires. English Heritage in the United Kingdom, the custodians of Stonehenge, still provides access for groups celebrating the solstice each summer.

Since the advent of modern science with luminaries such as Galileo and Copernicus, humankind has supplied scientific explanations for natural phenomena that previously could only be explained as the work of God. This has resulted in centuries of tension between the church and the world of science. Galileo was forced to recant his work during the Inquisition and spent the rest of his life under house arrest. The furor over Charles Darwin's theory of evolution continues to this day, more than 150 years after the publishing of *On the Origin of the Species.*

Today, physicists are attempting to put together a coherent theory that would explain the beginnings of the universe. Many on both sides of the religion/science debate have thought that this was an effort to someday put an end to the idea that God was "the author of the universe." But, a strange thing seems to be happening.

As the scientists attempt to reconcile the two branches of physics—quantum mechanics and classical physics—things begin to become really weird.

Although we don't seem to be closer to knowing what preceded the Big Bang, or what caused it, science does now tend toward the theory that it immediately created an instantaneous, massive expansion of our universe that quickly tapered off. Extrapolations of the expansion theory posit that the uneven tapering off of the expansion might well result in a possibly infinite number of other universes, or "multiverses." Instead of the three dimensions with which we are familiar, our universe may have as many as ten dimensions. Science is presenting us with whole new ways of looking at space, time, and reality.

One problem with all of the new science is that it may prove to be not only unsusceptible to scientific proof, but may lead us to a point at which it is incomprehensible to the human brain. Interestingly, this may bring us to a new juncture in the discourse between faith and science, one where we realize that we need to release God from the box of our human imaginations and instead imagine a much bigger God that is "beyond human knowing."

A Christian Perspective

Despite the (perhaps) pagan roots of celebrating the summer solstice, we can still celebrate the sun from a Christian perspective. After all, God created the heavens and the earth—all of creation! The ideas in this celebration explore the sun in the midst of God's creation, blending in a little science and stewardship of the earth along the way.

You may wish to take a scientific approach and talk about the compatibility with faith and science. Another helpful resource for older youth and adults is a series of videos (with an accompanying leader guide) entitled, *Faith and Science in the 21st Century* edited by Peter Wallace.[1] Or perhaps you want to simply focus on

---

1. Published by Church Publishing (2018). Available for download at *http://faithgoods.com/product/faith-and-science-download/*

the celebration of creation and the summer season with fellowship, prayer, some crafts, and a picnic.

Beyond the Celebration

Want to extend your observance of the summer solstice? Here are some suggestions:

- Research how the solstices are celebrated in the Southern Hemisphere.
- Arrange for members of a church in the Southern Hemisphere to be pen pals or Facebook friends with members of your church. Trade celebration ideas with each other and stay in touch throughout the year.
- Many of the activities provided for the Earth Day celebration (pages 1–23) would work well here too.

WORSHIP

Opening Prayer

Begin your celebration with one or more of the following prayers.

Almighty and everlasting God, you made the universe with all its marvelous order, its atoms, worlds, and galaxies, and the infinite complexity of living creatures: Grant that, as we probe the mysteries of your creation, we may come to know you more truly, and more surely fulfill our role in your eternal purpose; in the name of Jesus Christ our Lord. *Amen.*[2]

Heavenly Light, we praise you for this, the longest day of the year. As we move toward the solstice, we have more light day by day. After the solstice, we will have more darkness day by day. Thank you for being with us through light and dark. Thank you, too, for creation and the gift of light, physically through the sun, and spiritually through the Light of the World. *Amen.*[3]

---

2. "For Knowledge of God's Creation" in the Book of Common Prayer, 827.

3. From *She Who Prays*, 135.

CRAFTS

All of these projects focus on the sun and its effects: sunbeams, warmth, rainbows, and heat. Make sure you tie in the project with the summer solstice and how the sun is highest in the sky on this day, as well as it being the "longest" day of the year.

Rainbows and More Rainbows

Before doing this craft, learn more about rainbows. You can also add to your discussion the biblical incidences of when rainbows appear in the Bible study on pages 110 and 115.

Materials

- construction paper in all 7 colors of the rainbow (*Note:* From top to bottom they are: red, orange, yelllow, green, blue, indigo, and violet.)
- paint in the 7 colors of the rainbow
- fabric scraps in the 7 colors of the rainbow
- markers in the 7 colors of the rainbow
- scissors
- paintbrushes
- water
- rags
- glue or glue sticks
- 11" x 17" sheets of heavy paper
- *optional:* have a prism on hand to hold up to the light, and demonstrate the light forming a rainbow as the sun

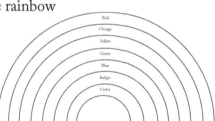

Directions

1. Explain to group members that they each will be making their own rainbow. Give them the option of either using paint, torn construction paper, fabric scraps, or markers (or a combination of all four, if they wish). *Note:* Markers will be the safest choice for youngest participants, who may just enjoy scribbling the colors on their papers.

2. Give each group member a sheet of paper.

3. Invite them to:

- Paint a rainbow, or . . .
- Tear pieces of construction paper and glue them on their paper to create a rainbow, or . . .
- Tear or cut the fabric into small pieces and glue together to create a rainbow, or . . .
- Use markers to draw a rainbow.

4. If possible, display the collection of rainbows in a public area for others to enjoy.

5. *Optional:* In advance, invite group members to bring fabric scraps or old worn out clothes and then have volunteers cut the fabric in small pieces. Draw a large rainbow shape on a piece of fabric, a sheet, or a tablecloth. Glue the small pieces of colored fabric onto the rainbow-shaped fabric to make a large rainbow wall hanging.

Sun Magnet

Make these as gifts or use them at home as reminders of God's good gifts of summer and the special activities and events we associate with summer.

Materials

- yellow and orange craft foam sheets (one each per participant)
- foam glue (available at craft and hobby stores)
- adhesive magnets strips or sheets
- sun shape pattern (*download at www.churchpublishing.org/faithfulcelebrations5*)
- scissors
- markers

Advance preparation (optional)

- Cut out the sun shapes from yellow foam sheets in advance.

Directions

1. Using the sun pattern, or creating your own, trace or draw a sun shape on the yellow foam sheet.
2. Cut out triangles or others shapes to glue onto the sun.
3. If desired, draw a face on the sun.
4. Stick a piece of a magnet on the back.

Sun Hats

Materials

- a variety of hats
- assorted decorations: stickers, feathers, sequins, glitter, felt and fabric scraps, etc. (This is a good activity for cleaning out your supply cupboard!)
- glue or glue sticks
- fabric markers
- needle and thread (for older children only)

Advance preparation

- Invite attendees to bring old hats, ball caps, etc. that they are willing to donate to be decorated during the celebration.
- Alternately, visit your local craft or hobby store for inexpensive plain caps, hats, or visors that are meant to be customized with your own decorations.

Directions

1. Distribute a hat to each participant. Assign helpers to the youngest participants to help them with selecting and attaching decorations to their hats.
2. The sky's the limit! Encourage creativity and invite participants to have at it. Who can create the wackiest hat? the prettiest hat? the most unusual hat?
3. Invite participants to wear their hats during your closing or to your "Summer Solstice Picnic," if you are having one.

STORYTELLING AND BIBLE STUDY

Creation Bible Study

Materials
- Bibles
- pens or pencils
- paper

Directions
1. Provide Bibles, pencil, and paper for participants.
2. Divide into smaller groups of 4–6 people each.
3. Ask for three volunteers *within each small group* to read the chosen scripture passage or story (see below for scripture suggestions) using this method:
   - Have the first volunteer read the passage aloud.
   - Invite group members to listen for and then each share a single key word or phrase that they heard in the passage that struck them as meaningful.
   - Ask the second volunteer to reread the passage aloud.
   - After the second reading, invite group members to share additional new words or broader insights into the reading.
   - Invite the third volunteer to read the passage a third time.
   - After the third reading, invite the group to share what they believe God is calling them to do or to share with others because of the reading.
4. Regather the larger group and invite a volunteer representative from each group to succinctly share their group's discussion.
5. Discuss together:
   - Where do you find yourself in the Bible passage(s)?
   - Where do you find this celebration's theme in the Bible passage(s)?

Select from the following scriptures
- Genesis 1–2: The creation story
- Ecclesiastes 3:1–8: "For everything there is a season . . ."

- Amos 5:8: God as Creator
- Psalm 74:15–16: God as Creator

Bible Study for Younger Children

For younger children, choose a Bible storybook or use the skills of a storyteller to tell the creation story (Genesis 1–2) or the story of Noah and the Ark (Genesis 6–8) at a level they can understand. You'll find several appropriate choices in the list found on page 111.

Materials

- Bible storybook or children's Bible
  - ○ The Story of Creation
  - ○ Noah and the Ark

Directions

1. If you tell the story of Noah and the Ark, ask wondering questions:

   - I wonder if the animals felt safe in the ark?
   - I wonder where *you* feel safe?
   - I wonder how you feel when you see a rainbow?

2. If you tell the creation story, ask the following wondering questions:

   - I wonder how the sun and moon create their light?
   - I wonder what is your favorite day?
   - I wonder how we can care for what God has created?

Note: Godly Play provides excellent stories for the above exercise. They can be found in *The Complete Guide to Godly Play, Volume 2, revised edition* by Jerome W. Berryman (Church Publishing, 2017).

Reading Corner

During your celebration, designate a quiet area for reading books about the sun and the summer solstice in small groups, individually, or with a storyteller.

The Summer Solstice by Ellen Jackson

Brother Sun, Sister Moon by Katherine Paterson

The Longest Day: Celebrating the Summer Solstice by Wendy Pfeffer

Midsummer: Magical Celebrations of the Summer Solstice by Anna Franklin

If Stones Could Speak: Unlocking the Secrets of Stonehenge by Marc Aronson

All Creatures Great and Small by Naoko Stoop

Noah's Ark by Lucy Cousins

Noah's Ark by Peter Spier

The Creation by Brian Wildsmith

The Children of the Morning Light: Wampanoag Tales as Told By Manitonquat by Manitonquat (Medicine Story) and Mary F. Arquette

To Everything There Is a Season by Jude Daly

If you choose to read any of the above as a group, discuss the following questions:

- What was your favorite part of the book?
- What did you learn that was new?
- What kinds of things do we make or do today to help us worship God?

If you selected one of the books on Stonehenge, discuss:

- How was Stonehenge made?
- Why?

MOVIE TIME

Watch one of the following films and discuss. Remember you need to have permission to view films in a church setting. Visit *www.cvli.com*.

Materials

- a method of projecting and viewing the film (for example, computer with digital projector; large-screen TV with DVD player)
- popcorn!

Directions

1. Select either a film or documentary episode.
2. Make sure the projection setup works and is ready to go.
3. Have discussion following the viewing.

Suggested films or documentaries

- *Brother Sun, Sister Moon.* This is a dramatization of events in the life of St. Francis of Assisi from before his conversion experience through his audience with the pope, including his friendship with St. Clare; directed by Franco Zeffirelli, from Paramount Studios. *www.imdb.com/title/tt0069824/*

- *The Fabric of the Cosmos.* A PBS NOVA series with physicist and author Brian Greene which can be viewed for free at *www.pbs.org/wgbh/nova/physics/fabric-of-cosmos.html.*

- *Journey to the Edge of the (Observable) Universe.* National Geographic presents the first accurate non-stop voyage from Earth to the edge of the universe using a single, unbroken shot through the use of spectacular CGI (computer-generated imagery) technology building on images taken from the Hubble telescope. *https://youtu.be/bVQpwxgMQCg*

- *NOVA: Secrets of Stonehenge.* Every year, a million visitors are drawn to the Salisbury Plain, in southern England, to gaze upon a mysterious circle of stones. Who built Stonehenge? What was its purpose? *www.pbs.org/video/nova-secrets-of-stonehenge/*

SCIENCE

A Human Sundial

On a sunny day in an open space with no shadows and no clouds overhead, driveways, parking lots, and playgrounds work well for creating shadows and doing an experiment using our bodies. Make sure you have enough space in all directions around you; shadows can grow long, and buildings often cover driveways as the day progresses. If there are trees or structures near the area you are considering, check the area in the morning, at mid-day, and in the evening to make sure that the area is not shadowed at any time of the day. You need the sun on the space to be able to trace shadows! This activity ideally takes place over time on a day when you know there will be no cloud cover.

Materials

- sidewalk chalk
- digital camera or phone camera
- tape measure
- pens or pencils
- paper

Directions

1. Split up in pairs and make sure everyone is spread far enough apart to make their human sundials. You will need about 20–30 feet between each pair.

2. Another option is to make one sundial using one person. Make sure you trace the same person throughout the day if you choose this option with everyone else taking turns doing the tracing.

3. Place an "X" on the spot that the person will stand each time or find some other way to mark the area in a way that will last all day.

4. Use sidewalk chalk to trace the person's shadow at least three times throughout the day: morning, mid-day, and late afternoon/early evening work great. Think of mealtimes as your cue to trace shadows, or set an alarm to go off. Every two hours

at 8:30 a.m., 10:30 a.m., 12:30 p.m., 2:30 p.m., and 4:30 p.m. gives a good sense of the movement of the sun.

5. Take photographs and record your observations on paper.

6. *Optional:* Ask questions during and after the experiment.

- How do you think shadows are made?
- What did you observe about your shadow and the sun?
- Did the sun move? If yes, which direction?
- In what direction did your shadow move?
- Are the tracings the same? Why or why not?
- When was your shadow the longest? When was it the shortest?
- Why do you think that your shadow changes throughout the day?
- Do you think that your shadow also changes throughout the year?

Learning About Rainbows

Use this information as part of your Bible study (page 110) or craft project (page 106).

A rainbow is a meteorological phenomenon that is caused by reflection, refraction, and dispersion of light in water droplets resulting in a spectrum of light appearing in the sky. It takes the form of a multicolored circular arc. Rainbows caused by sunlight always appear in the section of sky directly opposite the sun.

Rainbows span a continuous spectrum of colors. For colors seen by the human eye, the most commonly cited and remembered sequence is Isaac Newton's sevenfold red, orange, yellow, green, blue, indigo, and violet, remembered by the mnemonic *Richard Of York Gave Battle In Vain* (ROYGBIV). Newton, who admitted his eyes were not very critical in distinguishing colors, originally (1672) divided the spectrum into five main colors: red, yellow, green, blue, and violet. Later he included orange and indigo, giving seven main colors by analogy to the number of notes in a musical scale. Newton chose to divide the visible spectrum into seven colors out of a belief derived from those of the ancient Greek sophists, who thought there was a connection between the colors, the musical notes, the known objects in the Solar System, and the days of the week.

Rainbows can be caused by many forms of airborne water. These include not only rain, but also mist, spray, and airborne dew. Rainbows can be observed whenever there are water drops in the air and sunlight shining from behind the observer at a low altitude angle. Because of this, rainbows are usually seen in the western sky during the morning and in the eastern sky during the early evening. The most spectacular rainbow displays happen when half the sky is still dark with raining clouds and the observer is at a spot with clear sky in the direction of the sun.

We cannot talk about the significance of colors of the rainbow without mentioning the Bible. It is believed that "rainbow is a sign from the Almighty that we are not forgotten." After God appeared before Noah following the flood, there was a beautiful rainbow in the sky signifying God's glory and power as well as the covenant God established with Noah and all his descendants. Besides this account in Genesis, in Ezekiel 1:26–28, colors of the rainbow are compared to the glory of God. In the Revelation to John 4:3 and 21:11, the apostle John compares the rainbow colors to the glory or power of God.

FAITH IN ACTION

As Christians, we are called to be faithful stewards of creation, which includes addressing global warming and alternatives to fossil fuels such as solar energy. Learn how you and your family or community can make a difference and act toward sustainability. Invite an expert to come and speak with your group. Here are some examples:

Global Warming

Interfaith Power & Light (www.interfaithpowerandlight.org) is an organization with a mission to be faithful stewards of creation by responding to global warming through the promotion of energy conservation, energy efficiency, and renewable energy. They have chapters in every state and offer ideas and resources, plus will come and speak to a group about their work and ministry. (*www.inter faithpowerandlight.org/solar-state-by-state-resources/*)

Solar Power

Solar energy is gaining momentum around the world as more and more countries have begun transitioning to solar as a primal energy source. As the cost of solar energy has plummeted in recent years alongside major improvements in technical efficiencies and manufacturing quality, many homeowners and churches across the United States are starting to look at solar as a viable alternative energy solution.

Simply put, solar panels work by absorbing sunlight with photovoltaic cells, generating direct current (DC) energy, and then converting it to usable alternating current (AC) energy with the help of inverter technology. AC energy then flows through the home's electrical panel and is distributed accordingly.

To learn more about solar panels, solar energy, and how a family or church might explore tapping into this viable alternative for our buildings, invite someone who is an expert in the field as well as a provider of such installations to speak to your group.

RECIPES

Conclude your celebration of the Summer Solstice with a traditional summer picnic or simply share some refreshments during your event.

Sunspot Cookies

Even when the sun appears to be shining as brightly as ever to us, it sometimes has dark spots. These are called sunspots. They can happen when the magnetic field of the sun changes slightly in some places. These spots are a little colder and darker than the surrounding area. The sunspots can last for a few days or even a few months. During that time, they move across the surface of the sun and change in size, growing and shrinking as they go. But the sunspots eventually go away. However, these sunspots are delicious.

Ingredients

- ingredients for your favorite sugar cookie recipe (or use premade dough)
- 1½ cups powdered sugar (for icing)
- 3–5 teaspoons milk (for icing)
- flour
- mini chocolate chips, chocolate sprinkles, or finely chopped chocolate pieces for the sunspots
- yellow and red food coloring

Supplies

- circular cookie cutter about 2" in diameter
- bowls
- toothpicks
- rolling pin
- parchment paper
- cookie sheets
- wire racks

Directions

1. Sprinkle some flour over the counter or a cutting board and roll the cookie dough out with a rolling pin until it's about ¼" thick.

2. With your cookie cutter, or the rim of a glass, cut out your sun shapes.

3. Cut out as many as you can, then gather the dough and roll it out again. Cut out as many cookies as you can until you've run out of dough.

4. Place your cookies on parchment paper on a baking sheet and put them in the freezer while your oven preheats to 350°F.

5. Move the cookies straight from the freezer into the preheated oven. Bake for 10–12 minutes.

6. They should be just barely browned on the edges when they're done. Let them sit on the hot cookie sheet for a few minutes, then move them to a wire rack to cool completely. This takes about 30 minutes.

7. While the cookies cool, make your icing. Put the powdered sugar in a bowl and add the milk one teaspoon at a time.

8. After adding each teaspoon of milk, stir, stir, stir. If you added too much milk and the icing is too runny, add more powdered sugar. It's a very delicate balance, and it's very easy to add too much milk. You want it to be a nice, thick icing.

9. Split your icing between two bowls. Add 3 drops of yellow food coloring to the first bowl. Add 2 drops of red and 2 drops of yellow to the second bowl. Now you have your yellow and orange icing.

10. When the cookies are cool, spread yellow icing over the top with a butter knife.

11. Before the yellow icing hardens, drip some orange icing on top.

12. Use a toothpick to mix the two colors together. Gently drag the toothpick across the top of the cookie.

13. Try out different patterns and ways of moving the icing around.

14. Place a few chocolate chips, sprinkles, or other small chocolate pieces on top of your cookie. Look at those sunspots!

WORSHIP

Closing Prayers

Choose one or more of the following prayers or litanies (or those found on page 105) to conclude your celebration.

Canticle of Brother Sun

by St. Francis of Assisi

We praise You, Lord, for all Your creatures,
especially for Brother Sun,
who is the day through whom You give us light.
And he is beautiful and radiant with great splendor,
of You Most High, he bears your likeness.

A Litany of Praise

Leader: God of all power, Ruler of the Universe, you are worthy of glory and praise.

Participants: Glory to you for ever and ever.

Leader: At your command all things came to be: the vast expanse of interstellar space, galaxies, suns, the planets in their courses, and this fragile earth, our island home.

Participants: By your will they were created and have their being.

Leader: From the primal elements you brought forth the human race, and blessed us with memory, reason, and skill. You made us the rulers of creation.

Participants: Help us to be mindful caretakers of all that surrounds us in the sky, on the earth, and in the seas. *Amen.*[4]

---

4. Adapted from "Eucharistic Prayer C" in the Book of Common Prayer, 370.

Chapter 7

4TH OF JULY

INTRODUCTION

Each year on July 4, we celebrate our nation's birthday, the anniversary of the signing of the Declaration of Independence. This day also reminds us of the ongoing struggle to ensure that all Americans enjoy the rights enumerated in this historic document as they continue to develop since the nation's founding.

First, Some History

Also known as Independence Day, July 4th is a national holiday in the United States. On this day we remember the signing of the Declaration of Independence on July 4, 1776. Our nation's foundational document sets forth a bold, revolutionary vision for a new nation, with a statement that "We hold these truths to be self-evident, that all men are created equal, that they are endowed by their Creator with certain unalienable rights, which among these are life, liberty and the pursuit of happiness."

John Adams, one of the founding fathers and our second president, wrote the following to his wife Abigail: "The fourth day of July, 1776, will be the most memorable epoch in the history of America. I am apt to believe that it will be celebrated by succeeding generations as the great anniversary festival. It ought to be commemorated as the day of deliverance, by solemn acts of devotion to God Almighty. It ought to be solemnized with pomp and parade, with shows, games, sports, guns, bells, bonfires, and illuminations, from one end of this continent to the other, from this time forward forever more."

Eighty-seven years later Abraham Lincoln—at Gettysburg, Pennsylvania—invoked biblical language to remind his listeners that it had been "four score and seven years" since the founding fathers had put forth that bold vision for the new nation and "we are engaged in a great civil war, testing whether that nation, or any nation so conceived and so dedicated, can long endure." The idea that we could continue to exist half slave and half free had finally ripped the nation in two.

In 1869 the proposed Fifteenth Amendment to the U.S. Constitution, which gave the vote to black men following the Civil War, caused a split in the nascent movement to give that same vote to women. One group, led by such women's suffrage campaigners as Susan B. Anthony and Elizabeth Cady Stanton, refused to endorse the amendment, as it did not give the vote to women as well. Others, such as Lucy Stone and Julia Ward Howe, argued that the enfranchisement of black men would make giving the vote to women inevitable. In fact, it was another *fifty* years before the passage of the Nineteenth Amendment in 1920 secured the vote for all American women.

A century after the Gettysburg Address, our nation engaged in another monumental struggle in the fight for civil rights for the descendants of the slaves freed by Abraham Lincoln. Martin Luther King Jr. urged his people to employ the tactics of peaceful disobedience in the fight for freedom, to fight for the rights they were guaranteed in the Declaration of Independence, the Constitution, and the Bill of Rights. The dream of his famous "I Have a Dream" speech was that one day all citizens of the United States, including blacks, would share in the equality so nobly envisioned by our founding fathers. The movement culminated in the passage of the Civil Rights Act of 1964 and the Voting Rights Act of 1965.

Independence Day Today

In the more than two hundred years since the Declaration of Independence, our nation has come a long way in fulfilling the bold vision set forth by the founding fathers for a nation in which all people are created equal. It continues to be the model for freedom around the world. We have been and continue to be the envy of many. Our freedom and equality are very special gifts, to be celebrated, honored, and treasured. On this day we remember John Adams' hope that we celebrate with all our heart with cookouts, barbecues, parades, fireworks, prayers, and speeches that help us remember our story on this great anniversary festival.

But as we celebrate on this day, we should also remember the struggle that still continues for many who do not see equality under the law as well in their everyday life. The vision of our founders can only be complete when all of our citizens enjoy its benefits equally and to the fullest. In our Baptismal Covenant we promise to strive for justice and peace among all people and respect the dignity of every human being. This promise obligates us to continue to be open to the aspirations of all those who still find themselves short of full inclusion in our founders' vision.

Beyond the Celebration

- Many countries have an Independence celebration of one sort or another. You might research what different countries do to celebrate this precious freedom.

WORSHIP

Begin your celebration with the following prayer or litany.

Opening Litany

Leader: O Lord our Governor, bless the leaders of our land, that we may be a people at peace among ourselves and a blessing to other nations of the earth.

People: Lord, keep this nation under your care.

Leader: To the President and members of the Cabinet, to Governors of States, Mayors of Cities, and to all in administrative authority, grant wisdom and grace in the exercise of their duties.

People: Give grace to your servants, O Lord.

Leader: To Senators and Representatives, and those who make our laws in States, Cities, and Towns, give courage, wisdom, and foresight to provide for the needs of all our people, and to fulfill our obligations to the community of nations.

People: Give grace to your servants, O Lord.

Leader: To the Judges and officers of our Courts, give understanding and integrity, that human rights may be safeguarded and justice served.

People: Give grace to your servants, O Lord.

Leader: And finally, teach our people to rely on your strength and to accept their responsibilities to their fellow citizens, that they may elect trustworthy leaders and make wise decisions for the well-being of our society; that we may serve you faithfully in our generation and honor your holy Name.

All: For yours is the kingdom, O Lord, and you are exalted as head above all. *Amen.*[1]

---

1. "For Sound Government" in the Book of Common Prayer, 821–22.

CRAFTS

Fireworks Hats

Materials

- red, white, or blue cone-shaped paper hats (available from party and craft stores)
- 12" lengths of curly ribbon in red, white, blue, yellow, orange, purple, green, silver, and gold
- 4th of July decorations such as stars, glitter, small flag stickers, etc.
- scissors

Directions

1. Gather at least 18 ribbons in your choice of colors and knot them together on one end.
2. Take your cone-shaped hat and gently open the top pointy end (with scissors) to push your ribbons through *from the inside of the hat*.
3. Make sure that the knot is securely *inside* the point of the hat, then tape the knot to the inside side of the hat.
4. Take scissors and curl the ribbons. Your hat will look like fireworks!
5. You can decorate the outside of the paper hat with stars, glitter, small flag stickers, etc.

STORYTELLING AND BIBLE STUDY

Stories of Freedom

Using the Declaration of Independence, offer all ages an opportunity to share their own stories about what freedom means to them.

Materials

- copies of the Declaration of Independence, 1 per participant (download a printable version here: *www.constitution.org/us _doi.pdf*)
- copies of the Charter for Lifelong Christian Formation, 1 per participant (download a printable version here: *www.episcopal church.org/files/documents/charter_for_lifelong_formation_english _1.pdf*)

Directions

1. Read the Declaration of Independence while group members follow along. Discuss:

   - In what ways did the faith of the writers come through?
   - How does this document help us to respond to human need by loving service to seek to transform unjust structures of society?
   - How does this document help us to strive for justice and peace among all people, and respect the dignity of every human being? (*Baptismal Covenant*)

2. Invite everyone to share a story of how part of the Declaration has impacted their life.

3. Read the Charter for Lifelong Formation in the Episcopal Church. In what ways does the Declaration of Independence help us to do this work?

   - To develop new learning experiences, equipping disciples for life in a world of secular challenges and carefully listening for the words of modern sages who embody the teachings of Christ.

- By striving to be a loving and witnessing community, which faithfully confronts the tensions in the church and the world as we struggle to live God's will.
- By seeking out diverse and expansive ways to empower prophetic action, evangelism, advocacy, and collaboration in our contemporary global context.
- By holding all accountable to lift every voice in order to reconcile oppressed and oppressor to the love of God in Jesus Christ our Lord.

4. These points were as valid in that time as they are today. Discuss:

- How can we as Christians, through this Declaration, live into these points?
- What are we called to do?

Freedom Bible Study

Choose from the following scriptures, as appropriate for your group. Note that some stories will be appropriate for all ages; some may be challenging even for older participants. You could also consider reading a chosen story to younger participants from a children's Bible, including one with illustrations.

Materials

- Bibles (NRSV or children's Bibles, or both)
- pens or pencils
- paper

Directions

1. Provide Bibles, pen or pencils, and paper.
2. Begin with one of the selected scriptures.
3. Recruit three volunteer readers.
4. This first reader reads the passage slowly while remaining group members listen for a word or phrase that catches their attention. Ask each participant to write down this word or phrase.

5. Invite volunteers to share their selected word/phrase with the group.
6. The second reader then reads aloud the passage. This time, invite people to think and write about "Where does this passage touch my life? my community? our nation? our world?"
7. Invite each person who wishes to do so to share, beginning with the words "For me. . . ."
8. Ask the third reader to read aloud the passage. This final time, ask participants to ask themselves, "What in this passage is God asking me to *do* or *be*?"
9. Again invite volunteers to share their responses.
10. Repeat steps 3–9 with other scripture passages, if interest and time allow.

Select from the following scriptures
- Psalm 145
- Psalm 47
- Deuteronomy 10:17–21
- Isaiah 26:1–8
- Romans 13:1–10
- Hebrews 11:8–16
- Matthew 5:43–48
- Mark 12:13–17
- John 8:32
- 1 Peter 2:16

Another View of Freedom
Materials
- copies of the speech titled "The Meaning of July Fourth for the Negro," given by Frederick Douglass at Rochester, New York, July 5, 1852, 1 copy per participant (available at *www.history isaweapon.org/defcon1/douglassjuly4.html*)

Directions

1. Distribute copies of Douglass' speech.

2. Invite volunteers to take turns reading paragraphs of Douglass' speech, then discuss:

    • How would Frederick Douglass look at Independence Day today?

    • How would an ethnic minority person today look at Independence Day?

    • How did the Israelites feel about their loss of freedom and independence many times over in their history?

    • What are we called to do?

MUSIC

Hymns that recall and celebrate our freedom and our love for country are appropriate to incorporate throughout today's celebration of the 4th of July. Suggestions are offered below, but feel free to supplement these with your own favorites. Consider asking participants to identify their favorite patriotic songs, and make a point of including these as well.

You might also play stirring, familiar patriotic tunes, like marches by John Philip Sousa, "The Star-Spangled Banner" by Francis Scott Key, or "Over There" by George M. Cohan. Check your local library for recordings or visit iTunes or the Amazon.com MP3 store to purchase and download inexpensive MP3 versions of these songs.

Hymn Study

Materials

- hymnals such as *The Hymnal 1982*; *Wonder, Love, and Praise*; *Lift Every Voice and Sing II*; and *The United Methodist Hymnal*
- piano, guitar, or other instruments for accompaniment
- *optional:* recordings of patriotic music with CD or MP3 player
- *optional:* computer or tablet with internet access
- *optional:* assorted supplies for drawing/painting/sculpting; poster board, scissors, glue or glue sticks, tape or tacks

Suggested hymns

- "American the Beautiful" (#696, *The United Methodist Hymnal*)
- "My Country Tis of Thee" (#717, *The Hymnal 1982*)
- "Battle Hymn of the Republic" (#226, *Lift Every Voice and Sing II*)
- "Oh, Freedom!" (#225, *Lift Every Voice and Sing II*)
- "Free at Last" (#230, *Lift Every Voice and Sing II*)
- "A Song of Wisdom" (#905, *Wonder, Love, and Praise*)

Directions

1. Read or sing through one or more of these hymns. Discuss:
    - Which of these hymns are like prayers? like poems?
    - Can you find Bible passages to back up the words in the hymn?

2. Read about the author of the hymn (this information will easily be available online). Discuss:
    - What inspired them to write the words?
    - What impact have these words had throughout history?

3. If time and interest allow, invite volunteers to illustrate the hymn(s) using any of the available materials for drawing, painting, or sculpting. Or work together to create a collage illustrating a selected hymn.

4. Conclude by having a "Hymn Sing."

RECIPES

Flag Cake

Ingredients

- strawberries
- blueberries
- prepared sheet cake (boxed white cake mix or from one of your own recipes) frosted with white icing (or purchase a plain, frosted sheet cake from your local bakery or grocery store)
- ice cream

Supplies

- knives (*for adult use only*)
- serving and eating utensils, including plates
- *optional:* birthday candles and matches

Directions

1. Invite youth and adult participants to cut strawberries in half.
2. Taking a look at an American flag, place the strawberries to form the red stripes of the flag on the top of the cake, leaving space for the white frosting to show for the white stripes. (*Note:* Even the youngest of participants can do this step with guidance.)
3. In the upper left corner of the cake, use blueberries for the blue field leaving white spaces of icing showing through for the stars.
4. You may even like to put candles on the cake. It is our country's birthday after all!
5. Enjoy your cake with ice cream.

4th of July Ice Cream Social

You can hold this during your celebration or at its conclusion. If there are fireworks in your city or park with an area for everyone to gather, watch the fireworks together while eating ice cream.

Advance preparation

- Find out if your community (or one nearby) will be having a fireworks display. If so, consider the logistics of ending your celebration with an ice cream social just before the fireworks or at the site where they will be held.
- Plan the logistics ahead of time: transportation, meeting place, claiming your place to sit, transporting the ice cream and other needed materials, including those needed for cleanup, like plastic bags and wet wipes.

Supplies

- a variety of ice creams and toppings
- ice chests with plenty of ice
- serving and eating utensils, including ice cream scoops, cones, bowls, spoons, napkins, etc., preferably with a 4th of July theme
- *optional:* blankets for sitting, if attending a fireworks display
- *optional:* Fireworks Hats if created earlier in the celebration (page 124)

Directions

1. Communicate to potential participants where you'll be meeting and when. If this event is the conclusion of your celebration, you can share these directions as you're leaving the church. Otherwise, make this information known through your church's newsletter, website, or e-mail list. In this invitation, ask guests to bring their favorite ice cream (either homemade or purchased) and toppings.
2. Encourage group members to wear their Fireworks Hats.
3. This would also be a time to enjoy your "Flag Cake" (page 131).
4. Celebrate!

WORSHIP

Use one or more of the following prayers to conclude your celebration.

Lord God Almighty, you have made all peoples of the earth for your glory, to serve you in freedom and in peace: give to the people of our country a zeal for justice and the strength of forbearance, that we may use our liberty in accordance with your gracious will; through Jesus Christ our Lord, who lives and reigns with you and the Holy Spirit, one God, for ever and ever. *Amen.*[3]

Almighty God, who created us in your own image: Grant us grace fearlessly to contend against evil and to make no peace with oppression; and, that we may reverently use our freedom, help us to employ it in the maintenance of justice in our communities and among nations, to the glory of your holy Name; through Jesus Christ our Lord, who lives and reigns with you and the Holy Spirit, one God, now and for ever. *Amen.*[4]

Almighty God, who has given us this good land for our heritage: We humbly beseech you that we may always prove ourselves a people mindful of your favor and glad to do your will. Bless our land with honorable industry, sound learning, and pure manners. Save us from violence, discord, and confusion; from pride and arrogance, and from every evil way. Defend our liberties, and fashion into one united people the multitudes brought hither out of many kindred and tongues. Endue with the spirit of wisdom those to whom in your Name we entrust peace at home, and, that, through obedience to your law we may show forth your praise among the nations of the earth. In the time of prosperity, fill our hearts with thankfulness, and in the day of trouble, suffer not our trust in you to fail; all which we ask through Jesus Christ our Lord. *Amen.*[5]

---

3. "For the Nation" in the Book of Common Prayer, 258.
4. "For Social Justice" in the Book of Common Prayer, 260.
5. "For Our Country" in the Book of Common Prayer, 820.

Chapter 8

SUMMER CELEBRATION OF GOD'S CREATION

INTRODUCTION

"The world is charged with the grandeur of God," wrote Gerard Manley Hopkins, and Trinity Sunday—or any day in summer—is an excellent day to delight in that grandeur. Christians may be called a "people of the book," but they are also a people called to rejoice in God's good creation.

Creation: A Purposeful Act of a Loving God

This joy is part of our Jewish heritage. Many people are aware that the creation stories of Genesis are paralleled in the creation myths of other Mesopotamian peoples; fewer people are aware of what sets the biblical stories apart.

In Genesis, creation is no accident of an absent-minded god, but the loving intention of the One God. Nor are men and women created to be the slaves of the gods, but to be the crown of God's creation. Men and women are made to delight in the creation that delights its Creator.

This heritage of joy in the creation can also be seen in many of the psalms, such as Psalm 104, which praises God who makes "springs gush forth in the valleys," where wild donkeys "quench their thirst" (Psalm 104:10–11). Psalms 148 and 150 call upon the whole creation to respond to its Creator in praise: "Let everything that breathes praise the Lord!" (Psalm 150:6).

This loving response to the Creator is the special vocation of humanity, made in God's image. Dorothy L. Sayers, in *The Mind of the Maker*, shows that creative work itself is the response of love appropriate to humanity. Sayers points out that the story in which humanity is described as being made in God's image is a story in which God is shown doing only one thing: *creating*. Since God is Trinity, our own work as creators can be understood as a trinitarian activity. In other words, an understanding of the Trinity can illumine our understanding of creative work—and an understanding of our creativity can illumine our understanding of the Trinity.

The Creator in Us

Issues of creativity lie at the very heart of Christian formation, because to live a life of grace is to live creatively. Christians are not called merely to submit to a set of divine rules, still less to conform to the structures of an unjust society, but to remake the world into God's kingdom.

To help people become aware of themselves as creators, called to collaborate with the creative God, is a fundamental quest of Christian education. For children, this may be accomplished by inviting them to experience their powers as creators in a variety of media. For adults, these experiences may take second place to reflections upon experiences already gained.

But both adults and children will need to experience or recall the qualities of creative work found in a child's play. Watch a child at play, perhaps building a tower of wooden blocks. Their work is often distinguished by persistence, attentiveness, and painstaking care. This absorption in the work at hand rather than in the self is the quality that must characterize us as Christian workers and creators.

During the summer months, let us recover our sense of delight in God's creation. As we rejoice in this world of trees and sand, sidewalks, and manhole covers, let us rededicate ourselves to the work and play for which we were born. Let us remember our inheritance as creatures made in the image of God, who "saw everything that he had made, and indeed, it was very good" (Genesis 1:31).

Tips for Leaders

Several of the activities in this session are based on the idea of a Collection Walk, which invites participants to spend some time interacting with God's creation outdoors and collecting items to use for specific projects. This can work in urban, suburban, and rural settings, and you may choose to make this the focal point of your creation celebration. However, if you decide that this isn't appropriate for your group, there are many other activities included.

WORSHIP

Opening Prayer

Pray together Psalm 8 or sing together "For the Beauty of the Earth" (found in many hymnals).

Psalm 8

O Lord, our Sovereign,
how majestic is your name in all the earth!
You have set your glory above the heavens.
　　Out of the mouths of babes and infants
you have founded a bulwark because of your foes,
to silence the enemy and the avenger.
When I look at your heavens, the work of your fingers,
the moon and the stars that you have established;
what are human beings that you are mindful of them,
mortals that you care for them?
Yet you have made them a little lower than God,
and crowned them with glory and honor.
You have given them dominion over the works of your hands;
you have put all things under their feet,
all sheep and oxen,
and also the beasts of the field,
the birds of the air, and the fish of the sea,
whatever passes along the paths of the seas.
O Lord, our Sovereign,
how majestic is your name in all the earth!

CRAFTS

Psalm 104 Creation Mural

Materials

- Bibles
- masking tape
- roll of butcher paper, newsprint, or paper tablecloth
- scissors
- construction paper in assorted colors
- glue
- crayons and felt markers

Directions

1. Invite participants to make a mural illustrating Psalm 104. Divide participants into nine mixed-age groups. Distribute Bibles and assign each group a set of verses from Psalm 104:

   - *Group 1:* verses 1–4
   - *Group 2:* verses 5–9
   - *Group 3:* verses 10–12
   - *Group 4:* verses 13–15
   - *Group 5:* verses 16–18
   - *Group 6:* verses 19–23
   - *Group 7:* verses 24–26
   - *Group 8:* verses 27–30
   - *Group 9:* verses 31–34

2. Tape a long sheet of paper to a table or the floor, allowing 1'–2' of paper for each participant. If necessary, have each group make a separate mural.

3. Invite each group of participants to illustrate its set of verses using construction paper collages and drawings with crayons and felt pens. Hang the finished mural(s) in a public part of the building.

Creation Rubbings

This activity is designed to be used *during* the Collection Walk (page 149).

Materials

- paper
- crayons

Directions

1. Provide paper and peeled crayons to make rubbings on the Collection Walks.
2. To create a rubbing, place paper over an item with an interesting texture, then rub the flat side of the crayon over the paper, revealing the texture of the item underneath.
3. Interesting possibilities for rubbings include tree bark, man-hole covers, rocks, leaves, etc. If you create the Nature Collage (below), these rubbings can be included.

Nature Collage

This activity is designed to *follow* the Collection Walk (page 149).

Materials

- paper
- pens or pencils
- newsprint, butcher paper, or paper tablecloth
- markers
- glue
- tape
- items gathered on the Collection Walk
- photo printer for pictures taken during the Collection Walk

Directions

1. After participants return from their Collection Walk, divide into smaller groups of 5–6 members each (of mixed ages).
2. Give each group a large piece of paper.
3. Invite each group to make a collage of what they actually found on the walk.

Praise Mural

This activity is designed to *follow* the Collection Walk (page 149).

Materials

- newsprint, butcher paper, or paper tablecloth
- glue or tape
- markers or crayons
- materials gathered during the Collection Walk, including printed photos

Directions

1. After the walk, ask participants to make a mural titled *Praise God from A to Z.*
2. Invite the participants to decorate a long strip of paper with an alphabetical arrangement of items found on the walk, such as *acorns, bird feathers, cattails,* etc.
3. Use markers or crayons to fill in any missing letters and to decorate the border of the mural.
4. If possible, post the completed mural in a public part of your church or at home.

Sand Prints

This activity is designed to *follow* the Collection Walk (page 149), but could easily be completed with items brought into the session from your own yard or neighborhood park.

Materials

- natural materials for printing: rocks, leaves, flowers, etc.
- paintbrushes
- glue
- construction paper in assorted colors
- sand

Directions

1. Invite participants to make sand prints of items gathered from nature.

2. Demonstrate how to brush glue onto one side of the desired items and turn them, glue side down, onto a piece of colored construction paper. Press gently, and then carefully remove the item from the paper.

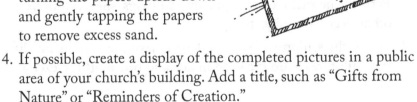

3. Sprinkle sand on the construction paper. Let the glue set the sand for several minutes before turning the papers upside down and gently tapping the papers to remove excess sand.

4. If possible, create a display of the completed pictures in a public area of your church's building. Add a title, such as "Gifts from Nature" or "Reminders of Creation."

Sand Casting

Invite participants to make sculptures cast in sand.

Materials

- sand
- water

- molds: empty milk cartons, cottage cheese containers, etc.
- plastic spoons
- twigs, shells, stones, other decorative objects
- either Plaster of Paris or paraffin/soy wax

Directions

1. Begin by mixing sand with water until moist enough to hold together. Put the sand into a mold, such as an empty milk carton.

2. Using hands or a plastic spoon, scoop out the sand leaving the shape desired for the sculpture or candle. This cavity will be filled with Plaster of Paris or wax.

3. Mix the Plaster of Paris with water or melt the wax over hot water. Help the participants fill their molds with the Plaster of Paris or the melted wax. Quickly add twigs, shells, stones, or other decorative objects.

4. When the sculptures have hardened, have the participants lift the sculptures from the sand molds and brush off the excess sand.

STORYTELLING AND BIBLE STUDY

The Creation Story

A *tableau* is a composition of people in a single, fixed position, comparable to a snapshot. A *pantomime* involves silent motion. Allow the group members to choose the medium of presentation that seems most appropriate for the events of their assigned "day" after hearing (or reading) the story of creation.

Materials

- Bible or children's Bible
- construction paper
- markers and/or crayons
- scissors
- tape and/or glue

Directions

1. Read the story of creation found in Genesis 1:1–2:4 to the participants, using a children's Bible, if possible.
2. Divide participants into seven groups of mixed ages. Invite each group to prepare either a tableau or a pantomime to illustrate one day in the creation story. The groups may use construction paper to make any props that will help illustrate the story (sun, moon, animals, plants, etc.).
3. Once the groups are ready, read the story again, asking each group to form its tableau or pantomime at your signal.

Genesis and John Bible Study

Materials

- Bibles
- paper
- pens or pencils

Directions

1. Distribute Bibles to participants. Ask one participant to read aloud Genesis 1:1–2:4.

2. After the reading, discuss the following questions:

   - How would you describe God the Creator in this story? (Consider asking each participant to give a one-word answer.)
   - How are man and woman different from the other creatures of God?
   - How are man and woman similar to the other creatures of God?
   - In what sense are we made like God or made in God's image?
   - How would you describe God's Word in this story?

3. Ask another participant to read aloud John 1:1–5. Discuss:

   - How would you describe God's word in this passage?
   - How does this story illumine the story of Genesis 1:1–2:4?
   - How does Genesis 1:1–2:4 illumine the story of John 1:1–5?

4. Divide participants into small groups of 4–5 members each. Invite each small group to write its own creation story that includes the insights of both Genesis 1:1–2:4 and John 1:1–5. When all the groups have finished, read the creation stories aloud for all to hear.

Creation Fables

This activity is designed to *follow* the Collection Walk (page 149).

Materials

- bags, boxes, or large envelopes
- items and photos gathered during the Collection Walk

Directions

1. Divide participants into small groups of mixed ages.

2. Ask each group to pick out three items from the walk and put them into a bag, box, or envelope.

3. Have groups exchange items, and then have each group make up a story using the found items as props or prompts for story-telling found in their bag, box, or envelope. Ideas might include how and why the item was created by God, what the "life story" of the item might be, and how the item "views" the world.

Bible Search

This activity is designed to *follow* the Collection Walk (page 149).

Materials

- Bibles
- Bible concordance

Directions

1. Select a few participants to find passages in the Bible that name items discovered during the Collection Walk and being incorporated into the activities following it, for example, trees, sand, weeds, water, people, animals, grass, etc.

2. As the other participants work on other activities, ask this small group to read the passages aloud.

3. For those unfamiliar with a Bible concordance, demonstrate its use.

GAMES

Creative Pursuit Game

Invite participants to play a game of "Creative Pursuit" to test their knowledge of God's creation and of the Genesis story.

Materials

- sheets of newsprint or scrap paper
- markers
- Bibles
- cake or other refreshment

Directions

1. Give each participant four sheets of newsprint or scrap paper. Ask each participant to number his or her sheets of paper from *1* to *4*. Divide participants into groups of 6–7 members each. Designate one participant in each group as *leader* and give each a Bible.

2. Ask each *leader* to stand in a fixed position with the other participants of each group forming a circle around their group's *leader*.

3. Ask each participant to use their sheets of paper to make a straight path to the *leader*, like the spokes of a wheel. Each path should begin with the paper numbered *1*, and end, next to the leader, with the paper numbered *4*. Each participant should begin by standing on their paper numbered *1*.

4. Beginning with one participant and moving in a clockwise direction, the *leaders* will ask each participant in his or her group a question about the creation story in Genesis 1:1–2:4 or a general question about God's creation. Tailor the questions to each participant, making them difficult or easy based on the person's age or knowledge of the Bible.

5. *Difficult questions might include*

- What did God create on the fifth day? (Genesis 1:20–23)
- What food did God provide for the wild animals and birds? (Genesis 1:30)
- What is the first verse of the creation story? (Genesis 1:1)

6. *Simple questions might include*

- What animal in God's creation says "meow"?
- Can you name a food from God's creation that is sweet?
- Can you name a flower in God's creation that is red?

7. If a participant answers correctly, invite that participant to step to the next paper on the path. When all participants in any one group are on the papers numbered *4*, the leader of that group calls out *Done!* The first group to finish wins the game, but if time and interest allow, let other groups finish as well.

8. Provide a cake or other refreshment for everyone. Ask the winning team to serve the cake to the other participants.

MUSIC

Praising God with Sound

Materials

- Bible

Directions

1. Read Psalm 150 aloud to the group. Explain that when this psalm was read aloud in the Temple, a pause after each verse was filled with the sounds named.

2. Ask participants to improvise a psalm of praise to God with sound. Begin by asking participants to think of loud noises that could praise the Lord: the roar of tigers, the clapping of hands, the crash of thunder, etc.

3. Then ask one participant to complete this sentence:

   - Praise the Lord with . . . [name a loud noise].

4. Invite other participants to imitate that noise as best as they can. Encourage a loud—even rowdy—game of praise to the Lord.

5. Ask another participant to complete the sentence with another sound. Continue for fifteen minutes or for as long as interest is sustained. Then conclude by reading the last verse of Psalm 150.

NATURE ACTIVITIES

Collection Walk

Before the celebration, read through the directions below and plan which activities will be done while walking, which activities will be done at a chosen location, and which activities will be done at your location before or after the walk.

Materials

- binoculars
- magnifying glasses
- digital cameras
- collection containers such as backpacks, envelopes, tote bags, or plastic grocery sacks

Directions

1. The general format suggested for the activities that follow is a collection walk—a walk during which participants collect sights, sounds, or specific items. You may prefer to plan the entire session for an outdoor location.

2. Activities for exploring three common items in our environment—trees, sand, and weeds—are included below. Here are tips and activities useful for any environmental exploration:

   - Give thought to a suitable location for your activities. Perhaps you have a beach or park available to you, or perhaps only an empty lot in the middle of the city. Help your participants celebrate the goodness of God's creation whatever your location.
   - Before the session, plan which activities will be done while walking, which activities will be done at the chosen location, and which activities will be done at the church before or after the walk.

- Do not distinguish between "natural" items, such as flowers and trees, and "manmade" items, such as manhole covers and fire hydrants. All creation is sustained by God—and most flowers and trees today have been planned, planted, and sustained by people.
- If you are exploring an urban environment, do not, for this session, focus on litter or signs of decay. Look for grass growing in the cracks of sidewalks, pigeons cooing on the ledges of abandoned buildings, and old bricks laid in intricate patterns.

- Useful materials on any walk include binoculars, hand lenses, magnifying glasses, digital cameras, and collection containers, such as backpacks, envelopes, tote bags, or plastic grocery sacks.
- Consider sending a few people out with an extra bag to pick up any litter they may find, as a service to your community.

Exploring Trees

1. Invite everyone outside to explore neighborhood trees. When you've found some suitable trees, discuss:
   - Put your arms around the tree. How far do your arms reach?
   - Smell the tree in different places: at the roots, on the bark, and at a leaf. What do you smell? Does it smell the same all over?
   - What lives in the tree? Check the branches, the bark, and the roots.
   - Can you make the shape of this tree with your body? How is one tree shaped differently from another tree?

Bird Feeders

Invite participants to make bird feeders to hang in trees either near the church or at home in their own yards or neighborhoods. Choose one or more of the methods offered below.

Materials (may not need all items on list, depending on which methods you select)

- plastic knife
- pine cones
- peanut butter
- bird seed
- string or yarn
- suet
- plastic mesh onion bags
- popcorn
- needles
- thread
- crumbs
- raisins
- cranberries

Directions for Method 1

1. Use a plastic knife to smear a pine cone with peanut butter.
2. Roll the cone in bird seed.
3. Tie string or yarn to the cone and hang on a tree branch.

Directions for Method 2

1. Melt suet over low heat.
2. Stir in bird seed until cool.
3. You may add peanut butter and crumbs if you wish.
4. Form the mixture into balls. Put one ball into each plastic mesh bag.
5. Tie string or yarn to the bag and hang on a tree branch.

WORSHIP

Closing Prayer

Close your creation celebration with one or more of the following:

Stand in a circle and sing the Doxology. Invite participants to close with a simple litany of thanksgiving. Ask them each to think of one blessing of creation for which they wish to give thanks. Go around the circle, allowing participants to name their chosen blessings of creation. Invite the rest of the participants to respond with the following phrase: "For [*chosen blessing of creation*] we praise you, Lord."

Sing "All Creatures of Our God and King" (*The Hymnal 1982*, #400; *The Presbyterian Hymnal*, #455; *The United Methodist Hymnal*, #62; *Evangelical Lutheran Worship*, #835).

Gather around the Creation Murals you made (page 138) and read together Psalm 148. You may choose to read it:

- in unison
- responsively, by dividing into two groups and alternating verses
- in choral fashion, going around the circle, each participant reading a line
- each group reading the section that describes its mural, and the whole group reading together the first and last line, "Praise the Lord!"